ONE CITY'S WILDERNESS

ONE CITY'S WILDERNESS
PORTLAND'S FOREST PARK

MARCY COTTRELL HOULE

SECOND EDITION

Twenty hikes in America's premiere urban forest.

OREGON HISTORICAL SOCIETY PRESS

Cover photo by Ron Cronin

This volume was designed and produced by the Oregon Historical Society Press

Library of Congress Cataloging-in-Publication Data

Houle, Marcy Cottrell, 1953–
One city's wilderness: Portland's Forest Park / Marcy Cottrell Houle
p.   cm.
Includes bibliographical references and index.
ISBN 0-87595-259-3
1. Hiking—Oregon—Portland—Guidebooks. 2. Forest Park (Portland, Or.)—Guidebooks. 3. Portland, (Or.)—Guidebooks. I. Title.
GV199.42.072H674   1995   917.95'49—dc20   95-42789

Printed in the United States of America.

This book is gratefully dedicated
in the memory of
Garnett (Ding) Cannon,
Dr. Arch Diack,
and Larry Espey,
for their vision, integrity,
and years of selfless work
for the protection of Oregon's
natural resources and parks
and also
to the members of Friends of Forest Park,
especially John Sherman,
for carrying on those ideals today.

The Oregon Historical Society would like to thank
FRIENDS OF FOREST PARK
NIKE
CITY OF PORTLAND
M.J. MURDOCK CHARITABLE TRUST
for their support of this volume and map.

CONTENTS

ACKNOWLEDGMENTS

I OWE SINCERE APPRECIATION to many people who have helped through the years to support the wide variety of research that went into this book. First, I wish to thank the "Oregon Parks Foundation" for funding the original grant that allowed me to conduct the first in-depth wildlife and botanical study of Forest Park. Special gratitude also goes to members of the Friends of Forest Park (especially to John Sherman), for their constant interest, support and vigilance on behalf of the park's welfare. Michael Casey of Nike also deserves a special thank you for his wonderful support of this book.

I am very grateful to Portland Parks and Recreation employees who care for Forest Park, the park's many volunteers, and the Portland Audubon Society, all of whom have been enthusiastic and extremely helpful for many years. A very special thank you goes to Fred Nilsen, for his careful reading of the manuscript and his time spent hiking and discussing the trails of Forest Park. A special thank you also goes to Fran Konig and Jim Sjulin, for the hours they spent going over maps and talking about the park.

Other individuals were always supportive, and I owe them a great deal: Carol Raines, for the long hours she spent on plant identification; Jean Siddall, for the thorough review of the Forest Park Plant Checklist; Glen Walthall, for the information he provided on Forest Park plants; Dr. R. Forbes, Tom McAllister, Chris Maser, and Harry Nehls, for sharing their expertise of the region's wildlife; Dr. John Allen, for reviewing the section on Forest Park geology; and Dr. Jerry Franklin, for the use of his map of vegetation zones of Oregon and Washington.

I am also indebted to the Oregon Historical Society Press for its wonderful help in putting this book in its final form. Special thanks go to Adair Law, managing editor, Christine Rains for her plant and animal drawings and for her maps of the twenty hikes, and Martha Gannett, who designed the beautiful new color map of Forest Park. Bruce Taylor Hamilton, Krisell Steingraber, and the late George T. Resch, also were instrumental in the original publication of this book.

And finally, my deepest and most loving thank you goes to my husband, John, and to my dear children, Emily and Jennifer, for their constant support and for always hiking and sharing in the fun of exploring the magnificent wonders of Forest Park.

INTRODUCTION

W HAT IS IT that makes Portland, Oregon, a leader among the cities of the nation in its appeal and livability? Part of the answer comes from its historical and cultural heritage and its outstanding natural beauty. And the culture, history, and beauty of an area are directly related to that area's natural history–from the vegetation, mammals, and birds that characterize it.

Close to the heart of downtown Portland lies a large, relatively undisturbed tract of land that captures the essence of what is natural and wild and beautiful about the Northwest–Portland's Forest Park. One of the largest city parks in the world, Forest Park stretches 7.5 miles long by 1.5 miles wide along the eastern slope of Portland's West Hills. Bordered on the south by Burnside Street, on the north by Newberry Road, on the west by Skyline Boulevard, and on the east by St. Helens Road, Forest Park's five thousand acres are an example of a western Oregon coniferous forest ecosystem. Hundreds of species of native Oregon plants and animals live and range within its borders. From this forest sanctuary, panoramic views of the city of Portland, the Willamette and Columbia rivers, and five major peaks of the Cascade Range–Mts. Rainier, St. Helens, Adams, Hood, and Jefferson–can be seen through the tall fir trees.

From its inception in 1947, Forest Park has been a refuge for both people and wildlife, and an integral part of the environment of Portland. It is the cool, green backdrop casting beauty to the city. It is part of the long, forested ridge known by the Indians as "Tualatin Mountain." This ridge, rising eleven hundred feet above the banks of the Willamette and Columbia rivers, stretches northwest from Portland, all the way to Oregon's rural

Coast Range, and links Forest Park with the natural habitat of that range. Presently free from urbanization, this forest corridor allows scores of native species of birds and mammals to freely traverse from the more wild areas into the city forest. The observer hiking among Forest Park's sixty miles of trails is rewarded by the sight of red-tailed hawks, great-horned owls, pileated woodpeckers, ospreys, black-tailed deer, raccoons, coyotes, beavers, and perhaps a bobcat while breathing the fresh air and enjoying the forest.

The purpose of this book is twofold: It is to be used as a descriptive field guide to the many beautiful trails of Forest Park, and also as an informative guide to the park's geology, history, vegetation, and wildlife. Comprehensive species checklists for Forest Park's plants, birds, and mammals are included in the book. Because Forest Park is a natural forest, a person learning about its plants and wildlife will be able to identify and understand the relationships of the natural flora and fauna of Douglas fir forests throughout western Oregon and Washington.

This new edition of "One City's Wilderness" has been thoroughly updated and also contains several important additions. A new, updated and easy to use map of the entire park is inserted in the back of the book. Bicyclists and equestrians will find valuable information on which trails, fire lanes, and roads in the park might be open for use. Bike and equestrian trails are dynamic, in that certain sections may be closed to allow them to "rest." Also, seven new hiking trails are described in detail to introduce the hiker to the beautiful but little used north end of the park. These hikes include two recently completed portions of Wildwood Trail. This remarkable, woodland footpath now spans 28.25 miles in length, making it the longest contiguous trail in a city park in the United States.

For its open space, recreational and educational opportunities, and exceptional natural beauty, Forest Park is unquestionably America's premier urban forest. Only minutes from a major, growing metropolis, this extraordinary place continually reminds us of our coexistence with the natural world, and at the same time saves for generations to come a priceless part of Oregon's heritage.

[Along the hills northwest of Portland] "there are a succession of ravines and spurs covered with remarkably beautiful primeval woods. . . . It is true that some people look upon such woods merely as a troublesome encumbrance standing in the way of more profitable use of the land, but future generations will not feel so and will bless the men who were wise enough to get such woods preserved. Future generations, however, will be likely to appreciate the wild beauty and the grandeur of the tall fir trees in this forest park . . . its deep, shady ravines and bold view-commanding spurs, far more than do the majority of the citizens of today, many of whom are familiar with similar original woods. But such primeval woods will become as rare about Portland as they now are about Boston. If these woods are preserved, they will surely come to be regarded as marvelously beautiful."

John Charles Olmstead
and Frederick Law Olmstead, Jr.,
Report of the Park Board
Portland, Oregon
1903

GEOLOGY

THE GEOLOGIC HISTORY of Forest Park has been a continuing drama predominantly characterized by several recurring themes: violent volcanic eruptions originating far to the east that flooded vast areas with thick basaltic lava flows; episodes when land surfaces were inundated and submerged by marine, lake, or river waters; periods of local volcanism; periods of faulting and folding; and, in between, long, relatively quiet periods when land building subsided and surfaces lay subject to erosion.

The oldest recorded geologic event in Forest Park began approximately twenty-two million years ago, during late Oligocene and early Miocene time, when the land area that would one day become the city of Portland was submerged underneath an inland embayment of marine waters. Thick beds of siltstone and shale, accumulating to depths of several thousand feet, were deposited under water at this time. This fossil-rich deposit, referred to by geologists as the "Scappoose Formation," is the oldest known formation underlying the West Hills of Portland and Forest Park. Deposition of the sediment ceased, however, when the entire region was slowly uplifted, forcing the seas to retreat. Over the next few million years, the area experienced a time of quiet and stability, and the sedimentary marine beds partly eroded. The calm of the period, however, belied what was about to happen in the east; an event which would, in retrospect, sculpt Tualatin Mountain more than any other single event in its history.

Sixteen million years ago, in middle Miocene time, intensive volcanic activity affected much of Oregon. Fissures in southeastern Washington and northeastern Oregon began erupting enormous quantities of fluid lava, sometimes pouring out hundreds of cubic miles of molten material that covered tens of thousands of square miles. As the lava cooled, it solidified and formed basalt, a heavy, fine-grained igneous rock. Vast plains of what geologists refer to as "Columbia River basalt" stretched from Idaho to the Pacific Coast. It flooded the Portland area, entering through an ancient Columbia River Gorge, and covered the underlying Scappoose Formation with over one thousand feet of basalt. Today, approximately seven hundred feet of Columbia River basalt underlie Tualatin Mountain, and constitute most of its bulk.

As Miocene time progressed, the eruptions stopped, and for several million years weathering forces attacked the basalt, slowly decomposing exposed, surface rocks into clay. During this period, the climate of the Portland area was tropical, and an extensive, reddish laterite crust, which is created under tropical conditions, formed on the exposed basalt.

Thirteen million years ago, another major disturbance rocked the region. At this time, the present-day Cascade and Coast ranges were uplifted, and the basalt land surface of Portland, which had originally been laid down nearly horizontally, was squeezed and folded. This rippling action formed valleys, geologically referred to as "synclines," that were separated by upfolded arches of layered rock, or "anticlines." This is evident in the ridge called Tualatin Mountain, which is an anticline that separates two major synclines to the east and west—the Portland and Tualatin valleys.

Between three and ten million years ago, during Pliocene time, the valleys continued to settle and eventually filled to become great lakes of water. The lakes, in turn, were filled with silts, today known as "Sandy River mudstone," that buried the basalt surfaces of the lake bottoms. When at last the basins could hold no more, they breached and joined with a powerful, ancestral Columbia River, which then rushed in to dump its load of quartzite pebbles and granitic rocks (carried all the way

3

from the Canadian Rockies) into the deformed, submerged valleys. These river deposits, known as the "Troutdale Formation," overlie the Columbia River basalt on side slopes in Forest Park at elevations of up to six hundred feet.

As Pliocene time drew to a close, volcanic activity resumed, this time, however, on a regional scale. Dozens of small, isolated volcanoes, generated by underlying source vents, rose up like exclamation points across the land surface of the Portland area. Referred to as "Boring volcanoes," they erupted lava, which cooled to become gray, platy basalt. Several such volcanoes existed along the crest of Forest Park, and poured out "Boring lava," a formation still visible in isolated sections along the ridge-top and on the western slope of Tualatin Mountain.

The final rock formation capping most of Forest Park was laid down during the last million years of Pleistocene time by the actions of two major forces, the river and the wind, working in tandem. The pulsing Columbia River, working to excavate a major river valley, was continually whipped by the wind, which over time picked up large quantities of yellowish-brown, clay-like silt from the Columbia's flood plain and transported it to the south and west. Today this wind-deposited silt formation, known as "Portland Hills silt," covers the upper part of most of the West Hills of Portland; its greatest known thickness of fifty-five feet occurs on Forest Park's crest.

Geologic sculpting of Forest Park still continues, with other forces influencing and altering its land configuration. Some geologists believe the eastern flank of Tualatin Mountain, a steep, straight, fifteen-mile ridge, is the result of a long fault that lies beneath present-day St. Helens Road. More recently modifying the surface of the West Hills of Portland, landslides have carved the major side slopes and over the past one hundred years have created major construction problems. Portland Hills silt, overlying Columbia River basalt, is an unstable formation when wet, and in an area of high seasonal rainfall, such as Portland, it has repeatedly proved to be a poor foundation material. Often landslides have resulted when the equilibrium of slopes blanketed by silt have been affected by excavation or construction. This seemingly detrimental condition, however, while causing chagrin in many an expectant and hopeful land developer, is a significant reason why Portland's Forest Park escaped development in the past and still remains in its lovely and natural state today.

HISTORY

THE EURO-AMERICAN DISCOVERY of the Willamette River in 1806 by Captain William Clark marked the beginning of interest and speculation in the fertile river valley that lay tucked away in a remote corner of the wild Oregon Territory. Twenty years later, spurred by the settlement of a Hudson's Bay Company headquarters in the region, pioneer travel up and down the Willamette River began. Permanent settlements soon dotted the landscape along the lower Willamette, beginning with the small communities of Linnton and Springville in 1843, and in 1845, with the establishment of Portland further upriver. Along the plains west of Tualatin Mountain, additional towns arose; and with them the desire of farmers to find ways to transport their crops to the people and shipping docks located along the Willamette River.

One geologic feature stood in their way, however—an eleven-hundred-foot forested mountain. The recorded history of Forest Park was set into motion.

The settlers were enterprising. Immediately they began to widen routes that had been used by Indians and explorers crossing Tualatin Mountain. By 1849, these primitive trails had turned into well-traveled passes, the names still used today: Germantown Road, Springville Road, Cornell Road, and Cornelius Pass. As the area grew more populated, parcels of forest land adjoining the roads were acquired by early settlers. By 1859, most of what is now Forest Park had been given away in Donation Land Claims and was quickly being logged. Wood from Tualatin Mountain was used for a variety of purposes—building materials, firewood, as well as fuel for steamboats coursing the river.

The vision of preserving what is today one of the largest city parks in the world began in 1867 with the arrival in Portland of Reverend Thomas Lamb Eliot, a Unitarian pastor educated at Harvard. For over thirty-five years, Reverend Eliot was dedicated to improving his chosen city. His dream was a Portland "enlightened"—a moral, humane place—and his labors quickly acquired for him the nickname "the conscience of Portland." By 1888, however, Reverend Eliot began fearing his vision was doomed to failure, seeing the Portland he loved quickly heading in a direction that he felt would cause it to become governed merely by accident or just another crossroad of struggling humanity.

Reverend Eliot increased his moralizing; it accomplished little. Not one to give up, he decided to initiate a new tactic—one that over the years would prove more successful than he ever could have realized—setting up a park system for Portland.

In 1899, at Reverend Eliot's persuasive insistence, the Municipal Park Commission of Portland was formed. He was appointed to its first board of commissioners, and, through his direction, the commission contracted the most important landscape architecture firm of its day, the Olmstead Brothers of Brookline, Massachusetts, to make a park planning study of the city of Portland. In 1903, John C. Olmstead came to Portland to conduct research and made several far-reaching suggestions. In their report, the Olmsteads planned for a circuit of connecting parks looping around the city—today known as the "40 mile loop." They also strongly suggested that the hills west of the Willamette River, now Forest Park, be acquired for a park of wild woodland character.

A "visit to these woods would afford more pleasure and satisfaction than a visit to any other sort of park," wrote the Olmsteads in their report. "No use to which this tract of land could be put would begin to be as sensible or as profitable to the city as that of making it a public park."

In 1907, voters approved a million-dollar bond issue to carry out the Olmstead plan. Unfortunately, most of the money went to developing existing parks, not to buying new ones. The plan to purchase Forest Park was set aside.

In spite of the setback, advocates for a "Forest Park" continued to increase. The head of the Bureau of Parks and Recreation from 1908 through 1915 was Emanuel Mische, who actively campaigned for a wooded parkway running along the West Hills. In 1912, E. H. Bennett, an eminent city planner brought out from Chicago to develop "The Greater Portland Plan," also remarked favorably in his report about the proposed park:

"A wide stretch of country and the Columbia River are seen from that proposed park on the North. . . . Deep splendid ravines and promontories from which the whole country with the distant snow-capped mountains come finely into view. . . . The forest reserves are extensive in the large cities of Europe. The great woodland areas are the great life-giving elements of the City."

Even with this accolade, again nothing was done to preserve the land for the proposed park. In 1913, a two-million-dollar bond issue was voted down, and a new city charter changed the organization of the park board. The Olmstead plan was filed away, and a disheartened Emanuel Mische, the ardent supporter of the plan, eventually resigned as park superintendent. Then, in 1914, the city of Portland started a wood-cutting camp on Tualatin Mountain to provide work for the unemployed.

At the same time, in hopeful anticipation of a great land boom, developers proposed and laid out large subdivisions throughout the proposed park. Thousands of lots were platted alongside imaginary roads. Richard Shepard, a realtor with great expectations, also promoted the building of a scenic drive contouring in and out of Tualatin Mountain's steep ravines, six hundred feet above the Willamette River. By 1915 the road, known today as Leif Erikson Drive, was completed, but the $150,000 cost was nearly twice as much as the developers and engineers had expected. In its first year, a winter's landslide closed the road, and engineers estimated that it would cost an additional $3,000 to repair the road.

It was a realtor's nightmare. To pay for the expense, the owners of the vacant lots were assessed. Consequently, between 1915 and 1931, hundreds of lots, totaling fourteen hundred acres, were forfeited to the city of Portland for nonpayment of the assessment. In addition, other land on Tualatin Mountain, after being logged off and burned by out-of-control slash fires, was forfeited to Multnomah County because of delinquent taxes.

Throughout these years, the dream to create a wilderness park still was held by many Portland citizens. One such person, Fred Cleator, of the regional foresters staff of the U.S. Forest Service and lover of the outdoors, led groups of the Trail's Club, the Mazamas, and the Boy Scouts in planting trees throughout the area to restore forest cover to the bare hillsides. The citizens' cause was given increased visibility when Robert Moses, a city planner of national reputation, came to Portland in 1943 to make the "Portland Improvement" report. A cogent item in his findings dealt with Forest Park:

"The City has not taken full advantage of its great
natural assets such as the wooded hills and river front.
Wooded hills and valleys in and around Portland have
in a large measure been overlooked, probably because
good scenery and forests are so plentiful in the Northwest.

"We believe that the steep wooded hillsides located
on the westerly border of the City should be in public
ownership.... The wooded hillsides west of the City
are as important to Portland as the Palisades of the
Hudson are to the city of New York."

Prompted by repeated demands that something be done to preserve the land as a park, Garnett "Ding" Cannon, an active Portland businessman, asked the City Club of Portland to conduct a study on the park's feasibility. Responding to Mr. Cannon's request, the City Club appointed a committee of five—John Carter, David Charlton, Allan Smith, Sinclair Wilson, and, as chairman, Garnett Cannon—to undertake the task. The committee's findings in a 1945 report unanimously confirmed the desirability of a six-thousand-acre, municipal forest-park "for the benefit of the community." The creation of such a park, they concluded, could provide the opportunity for several important objectives:

1. Provide facilities that would afford extensive nearby outdoor recreation for citizens and attract tourists.
2. Beautify the environs of Portland.
3. Provide food, cover, and a sanctuary for wildlife.
4. Provide a site on which youth and other groups could carry on educational projects.
5. Grow timber, which would in time yield an income and provide a demonstration forest.
6. Provide productive work for casual labor.
7. Protect the forest and exposed contiguous areas from fire, the slopes from excessive erosion, and the roads and lands below from rock, dirt, and other materials washed from the slopes.
8. Eliminate problems of unwise settlement and excessive public service costs.
9. Put idle public land into productive condition.

Because the City Club could not, under its bylaws, implement its own recommendations, the Federation of Western Outdoor Clubs, of which Cannon was president, began a program of action. In 1947, Cannon called a public meeting of citizens to formulate a plan to preserve the park. At this meeting the "Forest Park Committee of Fifty," a group of civic, commercial, educational, and recreational agencies, was formed. (This organization, presently called the Friends of Forest Park, is still active and concerned with all issues affecting the park.) Chosen as its first president was Thornton Munger, who had recently retired from the position of chief of research for the Pacific Northwest Forest Experiment Station.

Soon the public's attention was aroused; agreement was strong that the park be protected. Using this leverage, the Committee of Fifty petitioned the city council to dedicate all public lands in the area for park purposes, and, in addition, to adopt a policy to acquire private holdings within the designated six-thousand-acre boundary of the park.

In July 1947, the city council unanimously adopted the resolution. In May 1948, Multnomah County, after overcoming several legislative obstacles, transferred eleven hundred acres of land to the city park bureau without cost. The city of Portland also transferred fourteen hundred acres of land from the assessment collection division to the park bureau. Together, with additional gifts of land and other tax delinquent properties, a total of forty-two hundred acres of forest land was formally dedicated as "Forest Park" on 25 September 1948.

Today Forest Park spans five thousand acres. Acquisition of the remaining private lands within the designated six-thousand-acre boundary slowly continues to proceed. The vision of Reverend Eliot and the Olmstead Brothers, and the hard work and dedication of Garnett Cannon and other concerned citizens, has at last turned a far-fetched dream into reality.

VEGETATION

ON 4 APRIL 1806, while the Lewis and Clark expedition was returning eastward, William Clark made a side trip up the Willamette River; there he commented on the hillsides to the west and south of Sauvie Island, which today comprise Forest Park. Captain Clark reported:

"The timber on them is abundant and consists almost exclusively of the several species of fir already described [Douglas fir, grand fir, and western hemlock], and some of which grow to a great height. We measured a fallen tree of that species, and found that including the stump of about six feet, it was three-hundred-eighteen-feet in length, though its diameter was only three feet. . . . There is some white cedar of a large size, but no pine of any size."

As William Clark and Meriwether Lewis often would note in their journals, the trees of western Oregon were impressively abundant and immense. Today, scientists agree that the forests of the Douglas fir region of western Washington, western Oregon, and northern California are unique among all temperate forest regions in the world. A combination of factors, including the region's mild winters, dry, cool summers, the relative absence of hurricane-force storms, and the genetic potential of its tree species, make the area significant in three outstanding respects:

1. Species of coniferous or evergreen trees of the region (from the genera *Pinus, Abies, Pseudotsuga, Tsuga, Thuja,* and *Picea*) attain a greater age and size than those found anywhere else in the world.

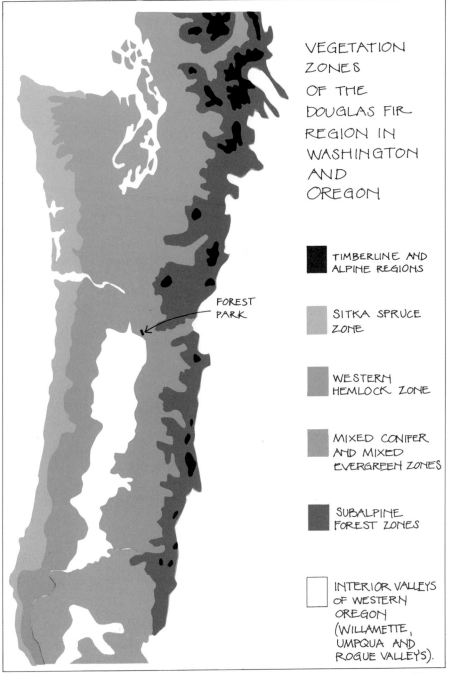

VEGETATION
ZONES
OF THE
DOUGLAS FIR
REGION IN
WASHINGTON
AND
OREGON

FOREST
PARK

TIMBERLINE AND
ALPINE REGIONS

SITKA SPRUCE
ZONE

WESTERN
HEMLOCK ZONE

MIXED CONIFER
AND MIXED
EVERGREEN ZONES

SUBALPINE
FOREST ZONES

INTERIOR VALLEYS
OF WESTERN
OREGON
(WILLAMETTE,
UMPQUA AND
ROGUE VALLEYS).

17

2. In terms of the sheer plant material, the forests of the Pacific Northwest have a greater accumulation of biomass, or living and decomposing vegetative matter, than any other temperate forest.

3. In its natural condition, the area is highly unusual in that it is dominated by coniferous trees.

In order to better understand the massive forests of the Pacific Coast, scientists have subdivided the region into specific areas that exhibit similar assemblages of plants and similar microclimates (rainfall and temperature). These vegetation zones are classified and named on the basis of an area's climax, or mature and self-perpetuating, vegetation. In western Oregon and Washington, the "Western Hemlock Vegetation Zone" encompasses the greatest area, and included within it is Portland's Forest Park. The western hemlock zone, in its natural, undisturbed condition, is forested primarily with three tree species: Douglas fir, western hemlock, and western red cedar. To a lesser degree, grand fir, black cottonwood, red alder, big leaf maple, madrone, and western yew trees also occur throughout the landscape. Shrubs are well developed; sword fern, salal, Oregon grape, lady fern, red huckleberry, vine maple, and western hazel are common and indicative species. Predominant wildflowers of the western hemlock zone include wild ginger, inside-out flower, Hooker's fairy bells, vanilla leaf, evergreen violet, and trillium.

Because Forest Park still remains in a semi-natural condition, it has maintained all of the western hemlock zone's naturally evolved, characteristic plants. However, one change is significant today. Instead of being dominated by evergreen trees, the park is clothed with a preponderance of red alder and big leaf maple trees. Much of the western hemlock zone, including Forest Park, has been extensively logged in the past 150 years. As a result, evergreen trees have declined appreciably, while hardwood species, mostly red alder, have proliferated.

Under natural situations, red alder is abundant only in streamside areas of the Northwest. In contrast, in areas where humans have imposed repeated disturbance to the natural vegetation, such as through intensive logging and brush fires, the soil becomes depleted of nutrients. Alder readily establishes itself under these conditions, sometimes choking out all the fir trees, unless the young evergreens have been seeded on the bare soil and gained a foothold concurrently with the encroaching alders. If Douglas fir does not get going at the same time with young alder, it will not compete as well, and may take a long time to grow into a stand.

When studying the vegetation of an area such as Forest Park, one needs to become familiar with the plants that presently occur, as well as the plants that have grown there in the past—and potentially will appear in the future. This is important, because a community of plants is not a static entity, but instead passes through a sequence of vegetative structures as it ages over time.

As a forest grows, it goes through several observable changes. After a major disturbance such as fire, the forest begins from bare ground and progresses in a relatively predictable manner to reach, after 250 or more years, a final, or climax stage. The series of conditions along the way are referred to by botanists as "successional stages," a term roughly analogous to the forester's expression "stand."

There are six successional stages in Forest Park. They are distributed as a mosaic throughout the park's forty-eight hundred acres, the patchwork scheme resulting from previous repeated logging activities and forest fires affecting different parts of the park. These successional stages are also observable in other parts of the western hemlock zone as well, and in order of progressing forest age are referred to as "grass-forb," "shrub," "hardwood with young conifer," "conifer topping hardwood," "mid-aged conifer," and, finally, "old-growth."

When one begins to comprehend how succession influences the vegetative landscape, suddenly the individual trees and shrubs observed in Forest Park take on new identity and meaning. There is a growing sense of a site's biological potential. In addition, by understanding succession, one gains a deeper appreciation of the complete interaction existing between plants and wildlife, because,

SUCCESSIONAL
FOREST SEQUENCE
OF THE
WESTERN HEMLOCK
ZONE

GRASS FORB	SHRUB	HARDWOOD WITH YOUNG CONIFER	CONIFER TOPPING HARDWOOD	MID-AGED CONIFER	OLD GROWTH
2-5 YEARS	3-30 YEARS	10-35 YEARS	30-80 YEARS	80-250 YEARS	250 YEARS

as will be explained in the "Wildlife" section, successional stages are directly related to the habitats of different species of birds and mammals.

The first successional stage of a forest, occurring two to five years after the previous vegetation has been removed by logging or fire, is the grass-forb stage.

This pioneering "forest" has a low profile—less than five feet tall—and contains no trees at all. Instead, it is identified by its numerous species of grasses and large patches of bracken fern, Canadian thistle, and fireweed. In Forest Park, the grass-forb stage makes up only one percent of the vegetation, occurring mostly along the park's firelanes.

When a forest is between three and thirty years old, the shrub stage becomes apparent. Red alder, big leaf maple, willow, bitter cherry, and Douglas fir trees begin to establish themselves at this time. But more noticeable, perhaps, is the variety of common shrubs which proliferate—thimbleberry, salmonberry, red-flowering currant, Indian plum, and several species of blackberry—all rang-

20

ing in height from two to twenty feet. In Forest Park, this stage covers approximately one hundred acres.

The third successional stage, hardwood with young conifer, is noticeable when a forest is between the ages of ten to thirty-five years. This stage makes up over twenty percent of the park and is recognizable by the presence of abundant alder and maple trees, twenty-five to seventy-five feet tall, with girths of eight to ten inches.

Alder, which is a common occurrence in northern Oregon and Washington, signals that the area has experienced disturbances in the past, for in the unlogged, unburned condition, a forest is predominantly made up of fir trees by this time. Under natural conditions, the soil is nutrient-rich and Douglas fir will dominate, while alder is restricted to the streambanks where it naturally occurs. Generally, the more alder that appears in a stand, the more disturbances the area has experienced in the past. In this successional stage in Forest Park, red alder and big leaf maple trees loom above the slower growing, juvenile Douglas firs and hemlocks. Sword fern, Oregon grape, red elderberry, and several species of blackberry are thriving shrubs.

Alder's reign does not last forever in a forest. When Douglas fir trees reach an age of approximately twenty-one years, they increase their annual growth rate, and by forty years of age, begin to actually exceed red alder in height. A forest between thirty and eighty years old, therefore, grows into the fourth successional stage, conifer topping hardwood. Because much of the park was logged between 1913 and 1940, making the forest approximately forty-five to seventy years old, this successional condition covers large areas of the park.

Fifth in sequence, comprising over fourteen hundred acres of Forest Park, is mid-aged conifer. This stage becomes noticeable when a forest has achieved the age of eighty to two hundred fifty years. Red alder, a tree that lives for only about one hundred years, has by this time grown old and is dropping out of the vegetative scheme. On the other hand, Douglas fir, which has a life span of more than seven hundred fifty years, is still young and thriving, and forms tall, stately stands; individual fir trees reach heights of ninety to one hundred forty feet tall, with trunks twenty-one inches or more in diameter. In the shadow of these firs grow a variety of shade tolerant plants—young western hemlock, western red cedar, and grand fir trees on drier sites. (These species will eventually dominate the climax forest when the Douglas firs grow old.) Sword fern, Oregon grape, red huckleberry, vine maple, and salal also flourish on the forest floor.

When a forest has escaped major disturbance for at least two hundred fifty years, the last successional stage of vegetation becomes established. This old-growth stage is self-perpetuating and will continue on and on, unless something forces it to be pushed back to an earlier condition. Past logging activities and substantial fires in Forest Park have reduced old-growth vegetation to almost nothing, but a few patches still occur in isolated locales near Macleay Park, Germantown Road, and Newton Road. These areas are set apart from younger stands by the virtue of several indicative structural features. Trees in the old-growth stage—predominantly western hemlock,

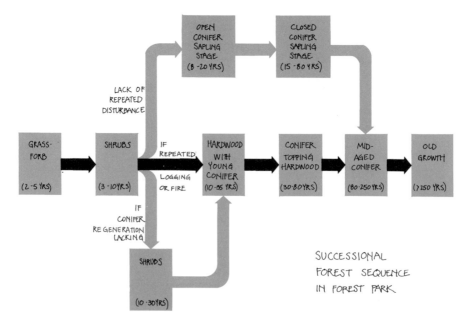

SUCCESSIONAL
FOREST SEQUENCE
IN FOREST PARK

western red cedar, and Douglas fir—are observably old and huge. Often they are individualistic in appearance, many sporting broken off crowns. Also present in abundance are large snags (standing dead trees), and dead and downed logs in various stages of decay. These last two features are apparent in mid-aged conifer stands, but not at the quantity found in old-growth. As will be further explained in the following section, snags and downed logs are necessary for many species of wildlife, which require them for breeding and feeding sites. They are also vital to the regeneration of the coniferous forest. Downed logs act as "nurse logs" for hemlock and Douglas fir seedlings, which establish themselves on the nutrient-filled trunks. (Alder rots too fast to become a nurse log.)

Old-growth areas play a critical role in the health of an ecosystem, for their giant trees hold within them rich gene pools that include characteristics such as longevity and the ability to ward off disease; traits necessary for the welfare and stability of future generations of trees. Too, the components of snags and downed logs, far from being signposts of a forest's demise, instead insure through their decay that life-giving nutrients are recycled back into the soil.

In essence, the sequence of successional stages in a forest follows a natural, progressive order. But what still must be considered is that a forest's development is influenced by a variety of other factors impinging upon it. Differences in soil characteristics and climatic conditions, the availability of sources of plant seed, and specific land management actions (logging, tree thinning, or planting, for example) all play a part in how a forest's vegetation will change over time.

When one unravels these secrets bit by bit, the seemingly disjointed parts suddenly unite to explain a fascinating, holistic picture of a living forest, such as Portland's own Forest Park.

KEY
N : Native
C : Common
DATES : Blooming Dates: January (1)–December (12), deciduous (D), evergreen (E)

COMMON NAME	SCIENTIFIC NAME	N/C	LOCATION	DATES
CONIFERS				
Douglas Fir	Pseudotsuga menziesii	N,C	Woods	—
Grand Fir	Abies grandis	N	Woods	—
Pacific Silver Fir	Abies amabilis	N	Woods	—
Western Hemlock	Tsuga heterophylla	N,C	Woods	—
Western Red Cedar	Thuja plicata	N,C	Woods	—
Yew	Taxus brevifolia	N	Woods	—
HARDWOOD TREES				
Big Leaf Maple	Acer macrophyllum	N,C	Woods	3-4
Bitter Cherry	Prunus emarginata	N,C	Woods	4-5
Black Cottonwood	Populus trichocarpa	N	Wet areas	4-5
Cascara	Rhamnus purshiana	N,C	Woods	5-6
Mountain Willow	Salix scouleriana	N	Open, damp areas	3-4
Oregon White Oak	Quercus garryana	N	Open areas	4-6
Pacific Dogwood	Cornus nuttallii	N	Woods	5-6
Pacific Madrone	Arbutus menziesii	N	Dry areas	3-5
Pacific Willow	Salix lasiandra	N	Woods	5-6
Red Alder	Alnus rubra	N,C	Woods, drainages	3-4
Sitka Mountain-ash	Sorbus sitchensis	N	Open woods	6-7
Sour Cherry	Prunus cerasus		Woods	—
Vine Maple	Acer circinatum	N,C	Woods	4-5
Western Crabapple	Pyrus fusca	N	Woods	5-6
Western Hazel	Corylus cornuta	N,C	Open woods	2-3
SHRUBS AND VINES				
Black Raspberry	Rubus leucodermis	N	Fields, woods	5-6
Blue Elderberry	Sambucus cerulea	N	Woods	5-8
English Holly	Ilex aquifolium		Woods	—
English Ivy	Hedera helix	C	Woods	—
Evergreen Blackberry	Rubus lacinatus	C	Open areas	5-8

WESTERN HEMLOCK
tsuga heterophylla

COMMON NAME	SCIENTIFIC NAME	N/C	LOCATION	DATES
Hawthorne	Crataegus oxycantha		Open woods	5
Himalayan Blackberry	Rubus discolor	C	Open areas	6-9
Indian Plum	Oemleria cerasiformis	N,C	Woods	3-4
Little Wild Rose	Rosa gymnocarpa	N,C	Woods	5-6
Nootka Rose	Rosa nutkana	N,C	Woods	5-6
Ocean Spray	Holodiscus discolor	N,C	Woods	6-7
Orange Honeysuckle	Lonicera ciliosa	N	Woods	5-6
Pacific Blackberry	Rubus ursinus	N,C	Meadows, woods	4-6
Poison Oak	Rhus diversiloba	N	Dry meadows	5-6
Red Elderberry	Sambucus racemosa	N,C	Woods	3-5
Red Flowering Currant	Ribes sanguineum	N,C	Open areas, woods	3-4
Red Huckleberry	Vaccinium parvifolium	N,C	Woods	4-6
Red-stem Ceanothus	Ceanothus sanguineus	N	Open woods	5
Salmonberry	Rubus spectabilis	N,C	Moist woods	3-5
Scotch Broom	Cytisus scoparius	C	Woods	4-6
Snowberry	Symphoricarpos albus	N,C	Woods	6-7
Thimbleberry	Rubus parviflorus	N,C	Open areas, woods	4-5
Western Clematis	Clematis ligusticifolia	N	Open woods	6-9
Western Serviceberry	Amelanchier alnifolia	N	Woods	3-5

GRASSES, SEDGES, RUSHES

COMMON NAME	SCIENTIFIC NAME	N/C	LOCATION	DATES
Common Rush	Juncus effusus	N	Damp woods	—
Field Woodrush	Luzula campestris	N,C	Open areas, woods	—
Henderson's Sedge	Carex hendersonii	N,C	Woods, fields	—
Oniongrass	Melica bulbosa	N,C	Woods, fields	5-6
Orchard-grass	Dactylis glomerata	C	Meadows	6-8
Reed Canarygrass	Phalaris arundinacea	C	Damp areas	6-9
Sweet Vernalgrass	Anthoxanthum odoratum	C	Meadows	5-6

FERNS, HORSETAILS

COMMON NAME	SCIENTIFIC NAME	N/C	LOCATION	DATES
Bracken Fern	Pteridium aquilinum	N,C	Open areas	D
Deer Fern	Blechnum spicant	N,C	Woods	D
Field Horsetail	Equisetum arvense	N,C	Wet areas	D
Giant Horsetail	Equisetum telmateia	N,C	Open areas	D
Goldback Fern	Pityrogramma triangularis	N	Rocks, open slopes	E
Lady Fern	Athyrium filix-femina	N,C	Woods	D
Licorice Fern	Polypodium glycyrrhiza	N,C	On trees	E

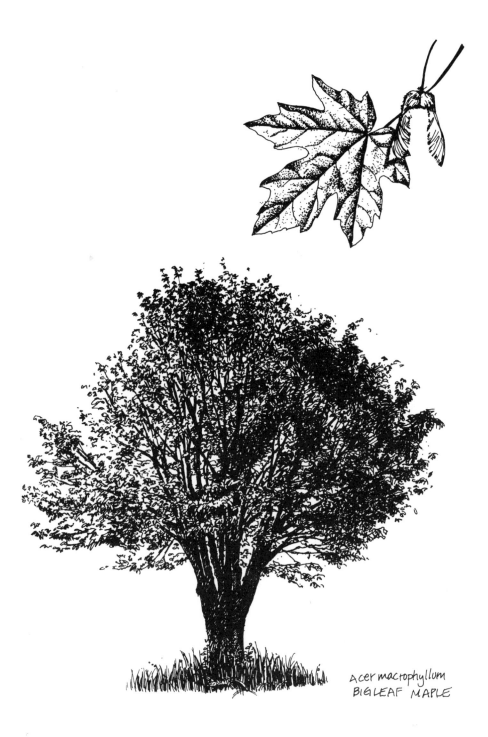

Acer macrophyllum
BIGLEAF MAPLE

COMMON NAME	SCIENTIFIC NAME	N/C	LOCATION	DATES
Northern Maidenhair Fern	Adiantum pedatum	N,C	Woods	D
Oak Fern	Gymnocarpium dryopteris	N	Moist woods	D
Spreading Wood Fern	Dryopteris austriaca	N	Woods	D
Sword Fern	Polystichum munitum	N,C	Woods	E

WILDFLOWERS

LILY FAMILY	LILIACEAE			
Clasping-leaved Twisted Stalk	Streptopus amplexifolius	N,C	Woods	5-6
Fairy Lantern	Disporum smithii	N,C	Woods	5-6
False Lily-of-the-Valley	Maianthemum dilatatum	N,C	Woods, stumps	5-6
False Solomon's Seal	Smilacina racemosa	N,C	Woods	4-5
Giant Fawn-lily	Erythronium oregonum	N	Woods	3-4
Hooker's Fairy Bells	Disporum hookeri	N,C	Woods	4-6
Star-flowered Solomon's Seal	Smilacina stellata	N,C	Woods	4-7
Tiger Lily	Lilium columbianum	N,C	Woods	6-7
Western Trillium	Trillium ovatum	N,C	Woods	3-4
IRIS FAMILY	IRIDACEAE			
Oregon Iris	Iris tenax	N,C	Meadows, roadsides	5-6
NETTLE FAMILY	URTICACEAE			
Stinging Nettle	Urtica dioica	N,C	Moist areas	4-6
BIRTHWORT FAMILY	ARISTOLOCHIACEAE			
Wild Ginger	Asarum caudatum	N,C	Woods	4-5
BUCKWHEAT FAMILY	POLYGONACEAE			
Western Dock	Rumex occidentalis	N,C	Moist areas	5-6
PURSLANE FAMILY	PORTULACACEAE			
Miner's Lettuce	Montia perfoliata	N,C	Woods	2-6
Narrow-leaved Montia	Montia linearis	N	Woods	2-5
Water Chickweed	Montia fontana	N	Wet areas	3-4
Western Spring Beauty	Montia sibirica	N,C	Woods	3-10
PINK FAMILY	CARYOPHYLLACEAE			
Starwort	Stellaria media	C	Meadows	2-9
BUTTERCUP FAMILY	RANUNCULACEAE			
Baneberry	Actaea rubra	N,C	Woods	4-5

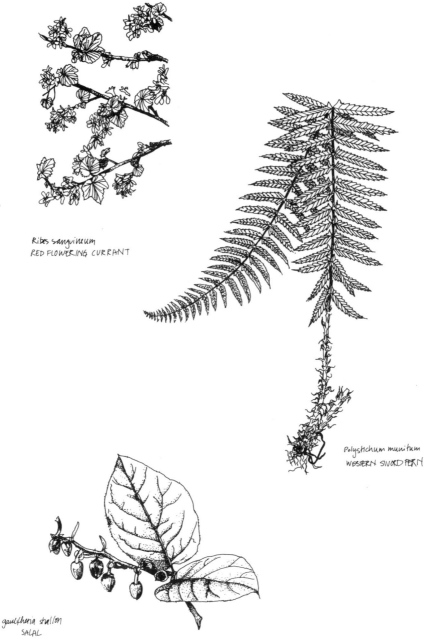

Ribes sanguineum
RED FLOWERING CURRANT

Polystichum munitum
WESTERN SWORD FERN

gaultheria shallon
SALAL

COMMON NAME	SCIENTIFIC NAME	N/C	LOCATION	DATES
Creeping Buttercup	Ranunculus repens	C	Damp areas	5-10
Little Buttercup	Ranunculus uncinatus	N,C	Moist areas	4-6
Red Columbine	Aquilegia formosa	N,C	Wood margins	4-9
Three-leaved Anemone	Anemone deltoidea	N	Woods	5-6
BARBERRY FAMILY	BERBERIDACEAE			
Cascade Oregon Grape	Berberis nervosa	N,C	Woods	3-5
Tall Oregon Grape	Berberis aquifolium	N	Open woods	3-5
Vanilla-leaf	Achlys triphylla	N,C	Woods	4-5
White Inside-out Flower	Vancouveria hexandra	N,C	Woods	5-6
BLEEDING-HEART FAMILY	FUMARIACEAE			
Wild Bleeding-heart	Dicentra formosa	N	Woods	3-6
MUSTARD FAMILY	CRUCIFERAE			
Angled-leaf Bittercress	Cardamine angulata	N	Woods	5-6
Cardamine	Cardamine pulcherrima	N,C	Woods	3-4
Silver Dollar Plant	Lunaria annua		Roadsides	4-6
Water Cress	Rorippa nasturtium-aquaticum		Wet areas	5-10
SAXIFRAGE FAMILY	SAXIFRAGACEAE			
Foamflower	Tiarella trifoliata	N,C	Woods	6-10
Fringecup	Tellima grandiflora	N,C	Woods	3-6
Leafy Mitrewort	Mitella caulescens	N	Woods	4-6
Small-flowered Alumroot	Heuchera micrantha	N	Woods, rocks	5-6
Western Golden Saxifrage	Chrysosplenium glechomaefolium	N	Wet areas	3-5
Youth-on-age	Tolmeia menziesii	N,C	Woods	4-7
ROSE FAMILY	ROSACEAE			
Goatsbeard	Aruncus sylvester	N	Woods	5-6
Large-leaved Avens	Geum macrophyllum	N,C	Woods	4-9
Steeplebush	Spiraea douglasii	N	Meadows	6-8
Woods Strawberry	Fragaria vesca var. bracteata	N,C	Meadows	4-6
PEA FAMILY	LEGUMINOSAE			
Giant Vetch	Vicia gigantea	N,C	Moist areas	6
Many-leaved Pea	Lathyrus polyphyllus	N,C	Woods	4-5
GERANIUM FAMILY	GERANIACEAE			
Bicknell's Geranium	Geranium bicknellii	N	Woods	5-8
Crane's Bill	Erodium circutarium	C	Trailsides	3-6

COMMON NAME	SCIENTIFIC NAME	N/C	LOCATION	DATES
Cut-leaved Geranium	Geranium dissectum		Trailsides	6-7
OXALIS FAMILY	OXALIDACEAE			
Oregon Oxalis	Oxalis oregana	N	Woods	3-5
VIOLET FAMILY	VIOLACEAE			
Evergreen Violet	Viola sempervirens	N	Woods	3-6
Johnny-Jump-Up	Viola glabella	N,C	Woods	3-8
EVENING PRIMROSE FAMILY	ONAGRACEAE			
Enchanter's Nightshade	Circaea alpina	N,C	Woods	5-7
Fireweed	Epilobium angustifolium	N,C	Roadsides, fields	6-8
PARSLEY FAMILY	UMBELLIFERAE			
Sweet Cicely	Osmorhiza chilensis	N,C	Woods	4-6
Water Parsley	Oenanthe sarmentosa	N,C	Wet areas	5-8
HEATH FAMILY	ERICACEAE			
Common Pink Wintergreen	Pyrola asarifolia	N	Woods	6-7
Indian Pipe	Monotropa uniflora	N	Woods	7-8
Salal	Gaultheria shallon	N,C	Woods	4-8
PRIMROSE FAMILY	PRIMULACEAE			
Western Starflower	Trientalis latifolia	N,C	Woods	5-6
MORNING GLORY FAMILY	CONVOLVULACEAE			
Field Morning Glory	Convolvulus arvensis	C	Meadows	5-9
WATERLEAF FAMILY	HYDROPHYLLACEAE			
Pacific Waterleaf	Hydrophyllum tenuipes	N,C	Woods	4-6
Small-flowered Nemophila	Nemophila parviflora	N,C	Woods	3-5
MINT FAMILY	LABIATAE			
Cooley's Hedge Nettle	Stachys cooleyae	N,C	Woods	7-9
Heal-all	Prunella vulgaris	N,C	Roadsides	6-9
FIGWORT FAMILY	SCROPHULARIACEAE			
California Figwort	Scrophularia californica	N,C	Woods	6-7
Common Mullein	Verbascum thapsus	C	Open areas	5-9
Common Speedwell	Veronica arvensis	C	Margins	5-6
Foxglove	Digitalis purpurea	C	Trailsides	7-8
PLANTAIN FAMILY	PLANTAGINACEAE			
Common Plantain	Plantago major	N,C	Meadows	6-9

COMMON NAME	SCIENTIFIC NAME	N/C	LOCATION	DATES
MADDER FAMILY	RUBIACEAE			
Bedstraw	Galium aparine	N,C	Cosmopolitan	3-7
HONEYSUCKLE FAMILY	CAPRIFOLIACEAE			
Twinflower	Linnaea borealis	N,C	Woods	6-8
SUNFLOWER FAMILY	COMPOSITAE			
Canadian Thistle	Cirsium arvense	C	Meadows	6-8
Coltsfoot	Petasites frigidus	N,C	Wet areas	2-5
Common Burdock	Arctium minus	C	Meadows, woods	8
Common Dandelion	Taraxacum officinale	C	Cosmopolitan	2-12
Common Thistle	Cirsium vulgare	C	Open areas	—
Common Yarrow	Achillea millefolium	N,C	Meadows	4-7
Oxeye Daisy	Chrysanthemum leucanthemum	N,C	Meadows	5-8
Tansy Ragwort	Senecio jacobaea	C	Roadsides	7-9
Trail Plant	Adenocaulon bicolor	N,C	Woods	6-8

WILDLIFE

OVER ONE HUNDRED TWELVE SPECIES of birds and sixty-two species of mammals can be observed living in or ranging through Portland's Forest Park. This diversity of wildlife, the majority of which are species native to the Northwest, is highly unusual when one compares this park with others in the nation's major cities.

In most large cities, urban development has resulted in an insidious but definite decline in the numbers of native birds and mammals. The usual progression of a city's expansion means that natural habitats disappear parcel by parcel, and that large, continuous, wooded areas are broken up by urban sprawl. Under these circumstances, native wildlife species are at a loss to respond and become trapped within limited pockets of available habitat, unable to migrate to more hospitable natural areas. What is the common result? Unfortunately, many naturally occurring species fall prey to local extinction with larger species that have more specialized requirements for breeding and feeding being the first to disappear—the native hawks, owls, and large woodpeckers.

For this reason, the majority of wildlife species in urban areas is non-native. Starlings, pigeons, house sparrows, Norway rats, and house mice proliferate in cities, these species finding no difficulty coexisting with humans. They readily migrate from other urban areas as native species decline.

Forest Park, however, makes Portland an anomaly among cities. Because of the park's exceptional size and, at present, its continuous, unfragmented habitat, large numbers of native birds and mammals live within it and thrive. More important in respect to wildlife, the park presently maintains a natural link with the habitat of Oregon's rural Coast Range. A corridor of natural vegetation connects the park's northwestern end to more wild, undeveloped areas. In effect, this acts like a funnel, allowing native animals to wander in and out of the park at will.

Taken together, these factors account for the continual presence of the kinds of wildlife observed by Lewis and Clark in the same vicinity. In 1806, Capt. William Clark commented on the animals he noticed in the forests along the Columbia River:

"We observe the marten, small geese, the small speckled woodpecker with a white back [hairy woodpecker], the blue-crested corvus [Steller's jay], ravens, crows, eagles, vultures, and hawks."

With the exception perhaps of martens, eagles, and ravens, these species can still be observed today in Forest Park. From a biological standpoint, it is important to remember that this assemblage of Northwestern animals is not random, but instead has evolved over centuries of time, owing to each animal's specific adaptations to its habitat. All wildlife species have requirements for breeding areas and feeding sites, and this results in wildlife and habitat being completely interrelated. Wildlife is *habitat*. The two cannot be separated.

Because wildlife responds primarily to the structural components of vegetation, the successional stages of a forest community can be thought of as habitats for wildlife. Early successional stages of a forest, with their low-growing profile and open conditions, attract animals adapted to these particular things. Later successional stages, which have many layers of vegetation, snags, and downed logs, attract wildlife that require these components. For this reason, a person walking through Forest Park or other low-elevation western Oregon and Washington forests can expect to see different assemblages of birds and mammals depending upon which successional stage of the forest that person is in.

Many of the species of birds and mammals found in

the older stages of a forest specifically require snags and downed logs for their breeding and courting sites and feeding stations. For example, woodpeckers are especially dependent on snags, needing those with sound wood in which to excavate their nesting cavities, and those more deteriorated to forage for insects. Woodpeckers are always important inhabitants in an ecosystem, because many species of animals requiring holes in trees for nesting sites (saw-whet owls, violet green swallows, tree swallows, chickarees, and northern flying squirrels) do not have the ability to carve holes for themselves; thus they are dependent on woodpeckers for drilling holes in snags for them.

Forest Park is able to sustain a variety of native wildlife species because of the many snags and downed logs distributed throughout its vegetation. This in itself makes the park unusual when compared to most city parks of the world. In other areas, snags, downed logs, as well as many species of native shrubs and trees, are cleared out in the effort to create "park-like" settings. This policy, however, is extremely detrimental to wildlife. By removing these necessary components, fewer places are left for the native wildlife to live, and the diversity of birds and mammals is sharply reduced.

When one observes the plants and animals found today in Forest Park, one must come to the inescapable conclusion that it is an outstanding example of a city park in terms of its naturalness. Only ten minutes from downtown Portland, one has the opportunity to observe eight native species of hawks, five species of owls, ten kinds of warblers, five types of woodpeckers, eight kinds of sparrows, and scores of other birds. One also has the chance to see coyotes, beavers, black-tailed deer, elk, black bears, and bobcats. What is impressive is that these animals are not in a zoo, but living in a semi-wild, semi-natural habitat, all within the confines of a city park—Portland's Forest Park.

BIRDS

Anna's Hummingbird
Barn Swallow
Blue Grouse
Brewer's Blackbird
California Quail
Golden-crowned Sparrow
Orange-crowned Warbler
Ring-necked Pheasant
White-crowned Sparrow
Willow Flycatcher
Yellow-rumped Warbler

MAMMALS

Beechey Ground Squirrel
Black-tailed Deer
Elk
Mazama Pocket Gopher
Red Fox
Spotted Skunk
Townsend Mole

Wildlife That Breed in the Early Successional Stages of Forest Vegetation (Grass-forb, Shrub, Hardwood with Young Conifer)

BIRDS

Black-capped Chickadee
Brown Creeper
Chestnut-backed
    Chickadee
Downy Woodpecker
Golden-crowned Kinglet
Great Horned Owl
Hairy Woodpecker
Northern Flicker
Northern Pygmy Owl
Northern Saw-whet Owl
Olive-sided Flycatcher
Osprey
Pileated Woodpecker
Red-breasted Nuthatch
Red-breasted Sapsucker
Sharp-shinned Hawk
Townsend's Warbler
Tree Swallow
Vaux's Swift
Western Flycatcher
Western Screech Owl
Western Tanager
Western Wood Pewee

MAMMALS

Big Brown Bat
California Red-backed
    Vole
Chickaree
Little Brown Bat
Long-eared Bat
Long-legged Bat
Northern Flying Squirrel
Red Tree Vole
Silver-haired Bat
Yuma Bat

Wildlife That Breed in the Later Successional Stages of Forest Vegetation (Conifer Topping Hardwood, Mid-aged Conifer, Old-growth)

Birds That Use Snags and Downed Logs for Nesting, Feeding, or Cover

SNAGS	DOWNED LOGS
American Kestrel	Bewick's Wren
Barn Owl	Blue Grouse
Bewick's Wren	Brown Creeper
Black-capped Chickadee	California Quail
Brown Creeper	Chestnut-backed
Chestnut-backed	Chickadee
Chickadee	Cooper's Hawk
Downy Woodpecker	Dark-eyed Junco
Great Horned Owl	Hairy Woodpecker
Hairy Woodpecker	Hermit Thrush
House Wren	House Wren
Merlin	Pileated Woodpecker
Northern Flicker	Red-breasted Nuthatch
Northern Pygmy Owl	Red-breasted Sapsucker
Northern Saw-whet Owl	Ring-necked Pheasant
Olive-sided Flycatcher	Ruffed Grouse
Osprey	Song Sparrow
Pileated Woodpecker	Steller's Jay
Purple Martin	Townsend's Solitaire
Red-breasted Nuthatch	Turkey Vulture
Red-breasted Sapsucker	White-breasted Nuthatch
Sharp-shinned Hawk	Wilson's Warbler
Tree Swallow	Winter Wren
Vaux's Swift	
Violet-green Swallow	
Western Screech Owl	
White-breasted Nuthatch	
Winter Wren	

Mammals That Use Snags and Downed Logs for Breeding, Feeding, or Cover

SNAGS	DOWNED LOGS
Big Brown Bat	American Shrew-Mole
Bobcat	Bobcat
Bushy-tailed Woodrat	California Red-backed
California Bat	Vole
Chickaree	Coyote
Deer Mouse	Creeping Vole
Little Brown Bat	Dusky Shrew
Long-eared Bat	Long-tailed Weasel

40

Long-legged Bat
Long-tailed Weasel
North American Black
    Bear
Northern Flying Squirrel
Opossum
Raccoon
Red Tree Vole
Short-tailed Weasel
Silver-haired Bat
Spotted Skunk
Striped Skunk
Yuma Bat

Marsh Shrew
Mountain Beaver
North American Black
    Bear
Northern Flying Squirrel
Opossum
Pacific Jumping Mouse
Raccoon
Red Fox
Red Tree Vole
Short-tailed Weasel
Spotted Skunk
Striped Skunk
Townsend Chipmunk
Wandering Shrew
White-footed Vole

COMMON NAME	SCIENTIFIC NAME	Forest Park Mammal Checklist
MARSUPIALS		
Opossum	Didelphis virginianus	
INSECTIVORES		
SHREWS		
Dusky Shrew	Sorex obscurus	
Marsh Shrew	Sorex bendirei	
Trowbridge Shrew	Sorex trowbridgei	
Wandering Shrew	Sorex vagrans	
MOLES		
American Shrew-mole	Neurotrichus gibbsi	
Coast Mole	Scapanus orarius	
Townsend Mole	Scapanus townsendi	
BATS		
Big Brown Bat	Eptesicus fuscus	
California Bat	Myotis californicus	
Hoary Bat	Lasiurus cinereus	
Little Brown Bat	Myotis lucifugus	
Long-eared Bat	Myotis evotis	

COMMON NAME	SCIENTIFIC NAME
Long-legged Bat	Myotis volans
Silver-haired Bat	Lasionycteris noctivagans
Western Long-eared Bat	Plecotus townsendi
Yuma Bat	Myotis yumanensis

RABBITS AND HARES

Brush Rabbit	Sylvilagus bachmani
Snowshoe Hare	Lepus americanus

RODENTS

MOUNTAIN BEAVERS

Mountain Beaver	Aplodontia rufa

SQUIRRELS

Beechey Ground Squirrel	Spermophilus beecheyi
Chickaree	Tamiasciurus douglasi
Northern Flying Squirrel	Glaucomys sabrinus
Townsend Chipmunk	Eutamias townsendi

POCKET GOPHERS

Mazama Pocket Gopher	Thomomys mazama

BEAVERS

North American Beaver	Castor canadensis

MURIDS

Black Rat	Rattus rattus
Bushy-tailed Woodrat	Neotoma cinerea
California Red-backed Vole	Clethrionomys californicus
Creeping Vole	Microtus oregoni
Deer Mouse	Peromyscus maniculatus
Dusky-footed Woodrat	Neotoma fuscipes
House Mouse	Mus musculus
Muskrat	Ondatra zibethicus
Norway Rat	Rattus norvegicus
Red Tree Vole	Arborimus longicaudus
Townsend Vole	Microtus townsendi
White-footed Vole	Arborimus albipes

JUMPING MICE

Pacific Jumping Mouse	Zapus trinotatus

COMMON NAME	SCIENTIFIC NAME
OAPROMYIDS	
Nutria	Myocastor coypus

CARNIVORES

DOGS	
Coyote	Canis latrans
Red Fox	Vulpes vulpes
BEARS	
North American Black Bear	Euarctos americanus
RACCOONS	
Raccoon	Procyon lotor
WEASELS AND ALLIES	
Long-tailed Weasel	Mustela frenata
Short-tailed Weasel	Mustela erminea
Spotted Skunk	Spilogale putorius
Striped Skunk	Mephitis mephitis
CATS	
Bobcat	Lynx rufus
Mountain Lion	Felis concolor

EVEN-TOED UNGULATES

DEER	
Black-tailed Deer	Odocoileus hemionus
Elk	Cervus elaphus

KEY TO RELATIVE ABUNDANCE

DURING NESTING SEASON—Spring and Summer
A : ABUNDANT (20+ birds seen or heard per day)
C : COMMON (5-19 birds seen or heard per day)
U : UNCOMMON (0-4 birds seen or heard per day)
R : RARE (may be years with no sightings)

ALL BIRDS DURING NONBREEDING PERIODS—Fall and Winter
A : ABUNDANT (50+ birds seen or heard per day)
C : COMMON (5-49 birds seen or heard per day)
U : UNCOMMON (0-4 birds seen or heard per day, or seen 5 or more times during season assuming observations are made regularly)
R : RARE (seen less than 5 times per season; may be years with no sightings)

COMMON NAME	SCIENTIFIC NAME	SP.	S.	F.	W.	NESTS IN PARK
HERONS						
Great Blue Heron	Ardea herodias	R	R	R	R	
SWANS, GEESE, DUCKS						
Canada Goose	Branta canadensis	U	R	U	U	
Mallard	Anas platyrhynchos	U	U	U	U	•
Tundra Swan	Cygnus columbianus	R	–	R	R	
Wood Duck	Aix sponsa	U	U	–	–	•
VULTURES, HAWKS, FALCONS						
American Kestrel	Falco sparverius	U	U	U	U	•
Cooper's Hawk	Accipiter cooperii	U	U	U	U	•
Merlin	Falco columbarius	R	–	R	R	
Northern Goshawk	Accipiter gentilis	R	R	R	R	
Osprey	Pandion haliaetus	R	R	R	–	
Red-tailed Hawk	Buteo jamaicensis	U	U	U	U	•
Sharp-shinned Hawk	Accipiter striatus	U	U	U	U	•
Turkey Vulture	Cathartes aura	U	U	U	–	

COMMON NAME	SCIENTIFIC NAME	ABUNDANCE				NESTS IN PARK
		SP.	S.	F.	W.	

PHEASANTS, GROUSE, QUAIL

COMMON NAME	SCIENTIFIC NAME	SP.	S.	F.	W.	NESTS
Blue Grouse	Dendragapus obscurus	R	R	R	R	●
California Quail	Callipepla californica	R	R	R	R	
Ring-necked Pheasant	Phasianus colchicus	R	R	R	R	
Ruffed Grouse	Bonasa umbellus	U	U	U	U	●

CRANES

Sandhill Crane	Grus canadensis	R	–	R	–	

GULLS

California Gull	Larus californicus	U	C	C	U	
Glaucous-winged Gull	Larus glaucescens	U	U	U	C	
Herring Gull	Larus argentatus	R	–	–	R	
Mew Gull	Larus canus	R	–	R	U	
Ring-billed Gull	Larus delawarensis	U	U	U	U	
Thayer's Gull	Larus thayeri	R	–	–	U	

PIGEONS, DOVES

Band-tailed Pigeon	Columba fasciata	C	C	C	R	●
Mourning Dove	Zenaida macroura	C	C	C	U	●
Rock Dove	Columba livia	R	R	R	R	

OWLS

Barn Owl	Tyto alba	R	R	R	R	●
Great Horned Owl	Bubo virginianus	U	U	U	U	●
Northern Pygmy Owl	Glaucidium gnoma	U	R	U	U	●
Northern Saw-whet Owl	Aegolius acadicus	R	R	R	R	●
Western Screech Owl	Otus kennicottii	U	U	U	U	●

NIGHTHAWKS, SWIFTS, HUMMINGBIRDS

Anna's Hummingbird	Calypte anna	U	R	U	U	●
Common Nighthawk	Chordeiles minor	–	U	–	–	
Rufous Hummingbird	Selasphorus rufus	C	C	C	–	●
Vaux's Swift	Chaetura vauxi	C	C	C	–	●

KINGFISHERS

Belted Kingfisher	Ceryle alcyon	R	R	R	R	

COMMON NAME	SCIENTIFIC NAME	ABUNDANCE				NESTS IN PARK
		SP.	S.	F.	W.	

WOODPECKERS

COMMON NAME	SCIENTIFIC NAME	SP.	S.	F.	W.	PARK
Downy Woodpecker	Picoides pubescens	C	C	C	C	●
Hairy Woodpecker	Picoides villosus	C	C	C	C	●
Northern Flicker	Colaptes auratus	C	C	C	C	●
Pileated Woodpecker	Dryocopus pileatus	U	U	U	U	●
Red-breasted Sapsucker	Sphyrapicus ruber	U	U	U	U	●

FLYCATCHERS

Hammond's Flycatcher	Empidonax hammondii	R	R	R	–	
Olive-sided Flycatcher	Contopus borealis	U	U	U	–	●
Western Flycatcher	Empidonax difficilis	C	C	U	–	●
Western Wood Pewee	Contopus sordidulus	U	C	U	–	●
Willow Flycatcher	Empidonax traillii	U	U	U	–	●

SWALLOWS

Barn Swallow	Hirundo rustica	C	C	C	–	●
Cliff Swallow	Hirundo pyrrhonota	U	U	U	–	
Northern Rough-winged Swallow	Stelgidopteryx serripennis	R	R	R	–	
Purple Martin	Progne subis	R	R	R	–	
Tree Swallow	Tachycineta bicolor	U	U	U	R	●
Violet-green Swallow	Tachycineta thalassina	C	C	C	R	●

JAYS, CROWS

American Crow	Corvus brachyrhynchos	C	C	C	C	●
Common Raven	Corvus corax	R	–	–	R	
Scrub Jay	Aphelocoma coerulescens	C	C	C	C	●
Steller's Jay	Cyanocitta stelleri	C	C	C	C	●

CHICKADEES, BUSHTITS

Black-capped Chickadee	Parus atricapillus	A	A	A	A	●
Bushtit	Psaltriparus minimus	C	A	A	C	●
Chestnut-backed Chickadee	Parus rufescens	A	A	A	A	●
Mountain Chickadee	Parus gambeli	–	–	–	R	

COMMON NAME	SCIENTIFIC NAME	ABUNDANCE				NESTS IN PARK
		SP.	S.	F.	W.	
NUTHATCHES, CREEPERS						
Brown Creeper	Certhia americana	C	C	C	C	●
Red-breasted Nuthatch	Sitta canadensis	C	C	C	C	●
White-breasted Nuthatch	Sitta carolinensis	R	R	R	R	
WRENS						
Bewick's Wren	Thryomanes bewickii	C	C	C	C	●
House Wren	Troglodytes aedon	R	R	R	–	
Winter Wren	Troglodytes troglodytes	C	C	C	C	●
DIPPERS						
American Dipper	Cinclus mexicanus	R	–	R	R	
KINGLETS, THRUSHES						
American Robin	Turdus migratorius	C	C	C	C	●
Golden-crowned Kinglet	Regulus satrapa	A	C	A	A	●
Hermit Thrush	Catharus guttatus	U	–	U	U	
Ruby-crowned Kinglet	Regulus calendula	U	–	U	U	
Swainson's Thrush	Catharus ustulatus	U	C	U	–	●
Townsend's Solitaire	Myadestes townsendi	R	–	R	R	
Varied Thrush	Ixoreus naevius	C	R	C	C	
WRENTITS, WAXWINGS						
Cedar Waxwing	Bombycilla cedrorum	U	C	C	R	●
Wrentit	Chamaea fasciata	R	R	–	–	
STARLINGS						
European Starling	Sturnus vulgaris	U	U	U	U	●
VIREOS						
Hutton's Vireo	Vireo huttoni	R	R	R	R	
Red-eyed Vireo	Vireo olivaceus	R	R	R	–	
Solitary Vireo	Vireo solitarius	U	U	U	–	●
Warbling Vireo	Vireo gilvus	C	C	U	–	●

COMMON NAME	SCIENTIFIC NAME	ABUNDANCE				NESTS IN PARK
		SP.	S.	F.	W.	

WARBLERS

COMMON NAME	SCIENTIFIC NAME	SP.	S.	F.	W.	PARK
Black-throated Gray Warbler	Dendroica nigrescens	C	C	U	–	●
Common Yellowthroat	Geothlypis trichas	R	R	R	–	
Hermit Warbler	Dendroica occidentalis	R	–	R	–	
MacGillivray's Warbler	Oporornis tolmiei	U	U	U	–	●
Nashville Warbler	Vermivora ruficapilla.	R	R	–	–	
Orange-crowned Warbler	Vermivora celata	C	C	U	–	●
Townsend's Warbler	Dendroica townsendi	C	R	U	R	
Wilson's Warbler	Wilsonia pusilla	C	C	U	–	●
Yellow-rumped Warbler	Dendroica coronata	C	U	C	U	●
Yellow Warbler	Dendroica petechia	U	U	U	–	●

TANAGERS, GROSBEAKS

COMMON NAME	SCIENTIFIC NAME	SP.	S.	F.	W.	PARK
Black-headed Grosbeak	Pheucticus melanocephalus	C	C	U	–	●
Evening Grosbeak	Coccothraustes vespertinus	C	U	U	U	●
Western Tanager	Piranga ludoviciana	C	C	U	–	●

SPARROWS, TOWHEES

COMMON NAME	SCIENTIFIC NAME	SP.	S.	F.	W.	PARK
Chipping Sparrow	Spizella passerina	R	U	R	–	●
Dark-eyed Junco	Junco hyemalis	C	C	C	A	●
Fox Sparrow	Passerella iliaca	U	–	U	U	
Golden-crowned Sparrow	Zonotrichia atricapilla	U	–	U	U	
Rufous-sided Towhee	Pipilo erythrophthalmus	C	C	C	C	●
Savannah Sparrow	Passerculus sandwichensis	R	R	R	–	
Song Sparrow	Melospiza melodia	C	C	C	C	●
White-crowned Sparrow	Zonotrichia leucophrys	U	U	U	R	●

BLACKBIRDS, ORIOLES

COMMON NAME	SCIENTIFIC NAME	SP.	S.	F.	W.	PARK
Brewer's Blackbird	Euphagus cyanocephalus	R	R	R	R	
Brown-headed Cowbird	Molothrus ater	C	C	U	R	●
Northern Oriole	Icterus galbula	R	R	R	–	

COMMON NAME	SCIENTIFIC NAME	ABUNDANCE				NESTS IN PARK
		SP.	S.	F.	W.	
FINCHES						
American Goldfinch	Carduelis tristis	U	U	*U*	*U*	●
House Finch	Carpodacus mexicanus	C	C	*C*	*C*	●
Pine Siskin	Carduelis pinus	A	C	*C*	*A*	●
Purple Finch	Carpodacus purpureus	C	C	*U*	*U*	●
Red-Crossbill	Loxia curvirostra	R	R	*R*	*R*	
WEAVERS						
House Sparrow	Passer domesticus	R	R	*R*	*R*	

"Forest Park represents an unparalleled resource where citizens can enjoy the peace, solitude, ruggedness, variety, beauty, unpredictability and unspoiled naturalness of an urban wilderness environment; a place that maintains this wilderness quality while allowing appropriate passive recreational and educational use without degrading natural resources; an urban laboratory for environmental research and resource enhancement and restoration; America's premier urban ancient forest."

Forest Park Natural Resources Management Plan
(Portland Parks and Recreation, 1995)

FOREST PARK TRAILS:
Introduction

A TRIP THROUGH FOREST PARK is both a pleasure and a privilege. The natural beauty, vast acres of
solitude, and the profusion of native plants and wildlife
all contribute to an exceptional woodland experience
rarely available to people inhabiting a major city. Forest
Park is not overrun with asphalt, swimming pools, picnic
areas, or developed sports fields. Instead, since its inception nearly a half century ago, it has offered a quiet
kind of enjoyment, the kind most cherished by all lovers
of the outdoors. The sixty miles of trails and fire lanes, the
old-fashioned, country feeling of eleven-mile-long Leif
Erikson Drive, and the hundreds of acres of hills and canyons in between, make Forest Park a haven for hikers,
bird watchers, nature photographers, runners, bicyclists,
equestrians, teachers, and students—in short, anyone
needing close-in inspiration and natural refreshment.

Because of all it offers, however, Forest Park runs the
risk of overuse in the face intensifying recreational demands. The 1995 Forest Park Natural Resources Management Plan—a comprehensive report drafted by Portland Parks and Recreation with the assistance of citizens
and technical advisory committees—has made the protection of its natural resources a central priority as it strives
to provide quality recreation use. To accomplish this goal,
the Portland Park Bureau has found it necessary to re-
strict some trails to single uses only, especially since many
trails are narrow and lack sufficient line-of-sight visibility
to safely allow multi-uses.

In general, all trails, roads, and fire lanes in Forest
Park are open to pedestrians. At the present time, twenty-
six miles of track are open to cyclists; this number is ex-

pected to increase after all the projects identified in the "Natural Resources Management Plan" are completed. Equestrians can enjoy numerous trails throughout the park.

Those trails, roads and firelanes specifically open for multi-use include the following: Leif Erikson, Saltzman, Springville, Newton, and BPA Roads, and firelanes 1, 10, 12, and 15, are available for pedestrians, cyclists, and equestrians. Firelane 3 is open to both pedestrians and cyclists, but closed to equestrian use. Firelane 7 allows both horses and hikers, but is closed to cyclists. Holman Lane may be used by both pedestrians and cyclists, but for visibility and safety reasons, bicycle traffic is limited to one way–uphill only.

Cyclists and equestrians using Forest Park should be aware that these stated routes may change over time if signs of overuse or user-conflict become apparent.

To provide a sampling of some of Forest Park's most beautiful areas, twenty hikes are described that cover most of the park's trails. Many of the hikes are loop trips, with the notable exception of the Wildwood Trail. For ease in hiking, Wildwood Trail is broken into seven sections and described as a one way trip. In many cases, side trails can be used to make these hikes into a loop. One-way trips require a vehicle at both ends. When beginning a one-way hike, be sure to take keys to this second car.

To reap the most enjoyment possible from a short or long outing in Forest Park, the hiker, cyclist, or equestrian should take several steps:

Take time to read through the hike you are interested in. A quick read-through can help answer many questions and ensure the hiker the maximum level of enjoyment and safety.

Be sure the car is locked and no valuables are left behind. When parking, be sure not to block any access roads, as they are used for emergency and maintenance purposes.

Pay attention to the weather. Even on sunny days, the temperature deep in the forest can be noticeably cooler and damp. Rain can surprise even the most experienced traveller anytime. Be prepared. Wear or carry warm clothes and rain gear.

Sturdy shoes are important; because of high seasonal rainfall, many trails during the year are apt to be muddy and slippery.

Carrying water on an outing lasting more than an hour or two is a good idea, for Forest Park's streams are not potable.

The picking of plants is not allowed. An important exception to this rule is the invasive plant, ivy. Ivy is the scourge of Forest Park. In places where it invades, ivy excludes native plants and shrubs and also prohibits the regeneration of native conifers, notably Douglas fir. Girdling ivy from tree trunks is one way to limit its menacing spread.

Camping, fires, and woodcutting of any kind are prohibited in the park.

Anything brought into the park must also be carried out. Litter and illegal dumping of garbage are an ongoing problem in Forest Park and ruin the aesthetics of the forest for everyone.

Motorized vehicles of any kind are prohibited in the park.

Forest Park's wild and natural character is what sets it apart from all other city parks in the nation. No other urban park in the United States offers anything comparable in quantity or quality. Learn to value and appreciate it. It's our treasure and what makes Portland different.

WILDWOOD TRAIL

World Forestry Center to
Macleay Park / MILE 0.0-5.0

DISTANCE: 5.0 miles (one way)*
HIKING TIME: 2½ to 3 hours (one way)
ELEVATION GAIN: 300 feet
ELEVATION LOSS: 450 feet
HIGH POINT: 900 feet
Foot traffic only.
One way trip; requires a vehicle at both ends of this hike.

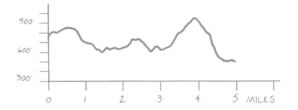

PORTLAND'S WILDWOOD TRAIL is one of the longest natural woodland trails winding through a city park anywhere in the United States. At 28.25 miles, this National Recreation Trail offers beauty and places of solitude, native plants and animals, and splendid enjoyment to outdoor enthusiasts, while being in close proximity to the core of a major city. For the purposes of this book and the ease of the hiker, Wildwood Trail has been divided into seven sections: Hike One describes the trail from just north of the Forestry Center through Hoyt Arboretum to Macleay Park (miles

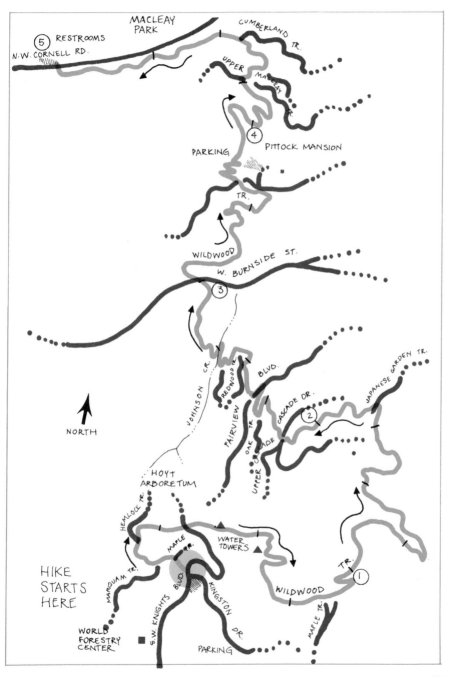

MACLEAY PARK

CUMBERLAND TR.

⑤ RESTROOMS
N.W. CORNELL RD.

UPPER MACLEAY TR.

④ PITTOCK MANSION

PARKING

TR.

WILDWOOD

W. BURNSIDE ST.

③

JOHNSON CR.

REDWOOD TR.

FAIRVIEW BLVD.

CASCADE DR.

JAPANESE GARDEN TR.

OAK TR.

UPPER CASCADE

②

NORTH

HOYT ARBORETUM

HEMLOCK TR.

MAPLE TR.

WATER TOWERS

WILDWOOD TR.

①

HIKE STARTS HERE

MARQUAM TR.

S.W. KNIGHTS BLVD.

KINGSTON DR.

MAPLE TR.

WORLD FORESTRY CENTER

PARKING

0.0 to 5.0); Hike Two, from Macleay Park to Firelane 1 (miles 5.0 to 11.25); Hike Three, from Firelane 1 to N.W. Saltzman Road (miles 11.25 to 16.0); Hike Four, from N.W. Saltzman Road to N.W. Springville Road (miles 16.0 to 22.5); Hike Five, from N.W. Springville Road to Germantown Road (miles 22.5 to 24.6); Hike Six, from N.W. Germantown Road to N.W. Newton Road (miles 24.6 to 26.3); and Hike Seven, from N.W. Newton Road to Firelane 15 (miles 26.3 to 28.25). Future plans include extending Wildwood Trail to the northwestern boundary of Forest Park at Newberry Road.

Milepost markers have been placed on blue-blazed trees at quarter-mile intervals along the entire trail and aid in locating the many side trails intersecting Wildwood. The trail is well-maintained and follows a gentle grade for most of its length, contouring through steep ravines at a level 750- to 850-foot elevation, making the hikes easy and pleasurable.

To reach the trailhead, travel toward Beaverton from downtown Portland via U.S. Hwy. 26 and take the Washington Park Zoo exit. Drive past the World Forestry Center—an educational attraction dedicated to explaining the forest industry and forest resources—and park in the lot at the intersection of S.W. Knights Boulevard and Kingston Drive. Notice the Oregon Vietnam Veterans Living Memorial also located near this intersection. Wildwood Trail starts across the street from the parking lot, just north of and up the hill from the Forestry Center.

WILDWOOD TRAIL begins in a woodland character, which it maintains for most of its 28.25 miles. Almost immediately, interesting spur-trails intersect with Wildwood (Maple Trail, Marquam Trail and then Hemlock Trail will intersect Wildwood), but throughout the hike, follow the signs for Wildwood Trail. After passing some ornamental trees and shrubs intermingled with native plant species, the trail crosses S.W. Knights Boulevard and continues up toward a water tower.

Continue on Wildwood, past Rose Trail and the first water tank. Just before Milepost ½ is a panoramic viewpoint with a sign denoting major landmarks: the Pittock Mansion and Mts. Rainier, St. Helens, Adams, and Hood. Cherry Trail branches right shortly thereafter. Continue walking beyond the Holly Trail junction, past a second water tank, and descend via several switchbacks into a ravine graced with plantings of ornamental fruit trees, in spring flowering with an abundance of fragrance and color.

At .85 mile, past the dual intersection of Cherry and Rose trails, Wildwood passes an open grassy area where many stop to picnic or rest. A short distance farther (immediately after Milepost 1), Wildwood drops into another meadow, which parallels Kingston Drive. The spot is a favorite with hikers and picnickers, for it is a wide-open, level area with picnic tables and plenty of space for Frisbee throwers.

The trail follows the edge of Kingston Drive about one hundred yards. After the meadow, Wildwood Trail climbs up and then down a small ridge where it becomes clothed once again in native shrubbery—Oregon grape, sword fern, and salal. Intermixed with the naturally occurring flora is an introduced, destructive species—ivy—escaped from home gardens.

Wildwood Trail makes a hard left switchback and then levels off. Near Milepost 1¾, look down the hill for a lovely view through the trees of the Japanese Gardens, regarded as one of the most authentic of this style of garden outside of Japan. The Japanese Garden Trail intersects Wildwood between Mileposts 1¾ and 2.

As the trail climbs away from the Japanese Garden area, halfway between Milepost 2 and 2¼ (passing Magnolia Trail), Wildwood Trail intersects with two paved roads, s.w. Upper Cascade and Cascade Drive. Cross the roads and continue up a relatively steep incline for .25 mile until the trail crosses Fairview Boulevard. (About halfway up the hill, just before the junction with Oak Trail, there is a park bench where a breather may be taken.) At Fairview, be sure to look behind for a stunning view of Mt. Hood. Cross Fairview Boulevard at the 2.4 mile mark of this hike, catching the connecting Wildwood Trail directly on the other side of the road.

Just before Milepost 2½, Wildwood Trail descends into an open park-like setting with many ponderosa pine trees growing alongside the trail. As the trail continues to drop down into the Johnson Creek canyon and passes Spruce Trail, its character soon changes; the trail reenters the forest and pines are replaced by densely planted sequoias—redwoods. (Watch for Wildwood's switchback to the right at the intersection with Redwood Trail.) Immediately after Milepost 2¾, Wildwood passes Creek Trail and crosses Johnson Creek. Cross the bridge and continue climbing for a short distance. Here Wildwood Trail will jog to the right, passing a connection with Redwood Trail, and head to w. Burnside Street, and then toward the Pittock Mansion, one mile away.

As the trail nears Burnside, fine examples of Columbia River basalt outcroppings are visible. Just past Milepost 3, Wildwood intersects with Burnside Street, a three-lane, heavily trafficked road; take great care crossing Burnside, and continue on Wildwood as it climbs steeply via switchbacks up the hill to the Pittock Mansion.

The trail crests the top of the hill after Milepost 3¾ and arrives at the Pittock Mansion parking area. The mansion is a Portland historic landmark originally built in 1914 by Henry L. Pittock, founder of the *Oregonian*. Today it is fully restored, open to the public, and administered by Portland Parks and Recreation. The overlook from the mansion is outstanding, showing the Willamette and Columbia rivers, five major Cascade mountains, and the city of Portland.

Wildwood Trail continues north across the parking lot of the mansion and for the next mile curves back and forth down a steep canyon. Just beyond Milepost 4½, Wildwood crosses Upper Macleay Trail, and after several more turns junctions with Macleay Trail to the right. Farther on, Cumberland Trail comes in from the right. Past Milepost 4¾, Wildwood Trail reaches N.W. Cornell Road. At the junction is a parking area and picnic site with tables and restrooms. Decide here whether to continue or stop, if other transportation has been arranged, and save the remaining 23.25 miles for other enjoyable hikes.

Cyanocitta stelleri
STELLER'S JAY

WILDWOOD TRAIL

Macleay Park to
Firelane 1 / MILE 5.0-11.25

DISTANCE: 6.25 miles (one way)*
HIKING TIME: 3 to 3½ hours (one way)
ELEVATION GAIN: 650 feet
HIGH POINT: 900 feet
Foot traffic only.
*One way trip; requires a vehicle at both ends of this hike.

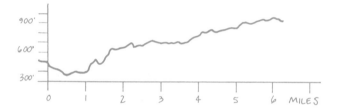

THIS SECOND SECTION of Wildwood Trail, bordering the Portland Audubon Society and winding through Macleay Park, is renowned for the giant old fir trees that line Balch Creek Canyon; it offers miles of gentle walking through mixed coniferous and deciduous forest.

To reach the trailhead, drive west on N.W. Cornell Road 1.7 miles from the intersection of N.W. 23rd and N.W. Lovejoy (Lovejoy becomes Cornell Road beyond N.W. 25th). Here there is a stone monument honoring Donald Macleay, who donated over one hundred acres of virgin forestland to the city as a park in 1897. Just beyond the sign is a turnoff

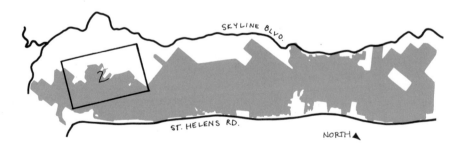

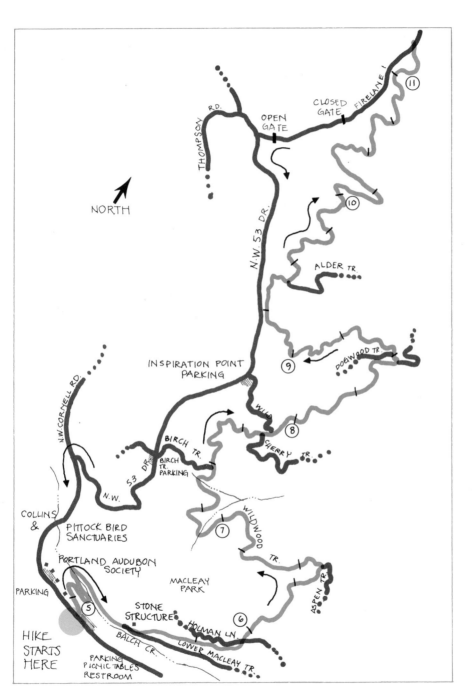

NORTH

THOMPSON RD.

OPEN GATE

CLOSED GATE

FIRELANE I

⑪

N.W. 53 DR.

⑩

ALDER TR.

DOGWOOD TR

⑨

INSPIRATION POINT PARKING

WILD

⑧

CHERRY TR.

N.W. CORNELL RD.

BIRCH TR.

BIRCH TR. PARKING

53 DR.

N.W.

WILDWOOD TR.

⑦

COLLINS &

PITTOCK BIRD SANCTUARIES

PORTLAND AUDUBON SOCIETY

MACLEAY PARK

ASPEN TR.

PARKING

⑤

STONE STRUCTURE

⑥

HIKE STARTS HERE

BALCH CR.

HOLMAN LN.

LOWER MACLEAY TR.

PARKING PICNIC TABLES RESTROOM

61

to the right where there is ample parking, as well as picnic and restroom facilities at the trailhead. Just north of this spot, and adjoining Forest Park, are the headquarters of the Portland Audubon Society and the Pittock and Collins bird sanctuaries, which together encompass more than one hundred acres of natural land devoted to the protection of wildlife.

BEGIN THE HIKE by following signs for Wildwood Trail (at Milepost 5), walking the path down a deep, heavily forested canyon known as Balch Creek Canyon. Balch Creek, which rushes through the bottom of this steep ravine, was named after Danford Balch, an early Oregon homesteader who, during a family quarrel, shot his son-in-law and was the first man to be legally hanged under Oregon law.

After several switchbacks, the trail crosses the creek at a bridge located at Milepost 5¼. Here Wildwood Trail begins to level off and numerous old-growth trees, some up to eighty inches in diameter at chest height, stand along the banks of the stream. At Milepost 5½, Wildwood meets Lower Macleay Trail at an old stone structure built by the Works Progress Administration (WPA); this building was a maintained restroom until it was heavily vandalized. Keep left on Wildwood (Lower Macleay Trail heads downhill to the right—see Hike Ten) and begin a 1.2-mile climb out of the canyon. There are several crude, log park benches spread along this hike, the first of which can be found at Milepost 6¼ (others are near Mileposts 9¾, 10¼, and between 10½ and 10¾). Beyond Milepost 6¼, Aspen Trail (see Hike Nine) merges from the right. After a substantial climb, the trail finally levels off at Milepost 6¾. From this point on, Wildwood generally stays at a 700- to 850-foot elevation for the remainder of its length.

Much of the trail from Mileposts 7 to 11 is in a mid-successional forest state—the conifer topping hardwood stage. Eventually, if left undisturbed, most of the deciduous trees will reach their climax age and will die out and be replaced by Douglas fir, western red cedar, and western hemlock. Presently, because of the abundance of alder and maple trees, many birds are attracted to this area in spring to feast on the deciduous trees' catkins. Look for warblers, evening grosbeaks, pine siskins, and listen for chickadees and red-breasted nuthatches, especially from April through June. Also be on the watch for red-tailed hawks and turkey vultures, birds of prey that seem to enjoy this section of Forest Park.

62

Between Mileposts 7 and 10, several spur trails adjoin Wildwood (Birch Trail, Wild Cherry Trail, Dogwood Trail, and Alder Trail intersect Wildwood on this three-mile stretch). These trails are discussed elsewhere in this book. For this hike, stay on Wildwood Trail and wind in and out of ravines, crossing a number of footbridges.

In the section between Mileposts 7¼ and 8¼, a man-made ditch parallels the trail to the left. This ditch was dug in the early 1900s to bring water from the other side of Tualatin Mountain to hydraulically sluice out Westover Terrace (located below the park) for homesites. Because of the excess moisture trapped in this area, many cottonwood trees, which require more water, grow along the side of the trail. In summer, these trees are identifiable by their deltoid leaves, and in winter by their deeply furrowed bark.

Care must be taken on Wildwood between Mileposts 7¼ and 8¼. Here, hikers and runners will find many hard tree roots exposed on the trail's surface. It is easy to trip in this section, especially during the spring and summer months when ground-level foliage drapes over the trail.

Close to Milepost 9¼, the trail reaches the entrance from N.W. 53rd; this is a popular starting point for hikers and joggers. A short distance farther, between Mileposts 9¼ and 9½, Alder Trail heads downhill to the right.

Near Milepost 10¼, there is a pocket of older coniferous trees interspersed with a variety of snags evidencing numerous woodpecker holes. The wild cry of a pileated woodpecker, the largest woodpecker native to western Oregon, is often heard near this point. These birds play a tremendously important role in a forest ecosystem. Because they are insectivorous, they exert constant pressure on native insect populations, which helps prevent insects from reaching epidemic levels. For example, woodpeckers will consume twenty-four to ninety-eight percent of a beetle population at moderate to high beetle densities.

The forest opens up again near Milepost 10¾ and remains dominated by deciduous trees. Beyond Milepost 11, Wildwood Trail crosses Firelane 1. Here there is an open meadow for resting, and a perfect spot to decide whether to continue on the next six-mile segment, which leads deep to the core of Forest Park. To complete this hike, walk .3 mile up Firelane 1 to the second vehicle parked at the locked gate.

WILDWOOD TRAIL

Firelane 1 to
N.W. Saltzman Road / MILE 11.25-16.0

DISTANCE: 4.75 miles (one way)*
HIKING TIME: 2½ hours (one way)
ELEVATION GAIN: 200 feet
HIGH POINT: 900 feet
Foot traffic only.
One way trip; requires a vehicle at both ends of this hike.

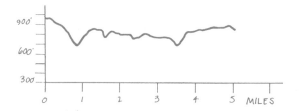

THIS PORTION of Wildwood Trail is one of the most scenic and rewarding of all the hikes described in this book, for it takes the hiker into the deep, central section of Forest Park, far from roads or houses. The woods are quiet and offer exceptional stands of older coniferous forest.

To reach the beginning of the hike, drive west 2.2 miles from the intersection of N.W. 23rd and N.W. Lovejoy along N.W. Cornell Road (Lovejoy becomes N.W. Cornell Road beyond N.W. 25th) until it intersects with N.W. 53rd Drive. Turn right on N.W. 53rd Drive and follow it for 1.7 miles, then turn right again on N.W. Forest Lane (Firelane 1),

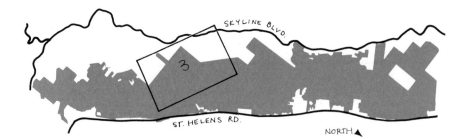

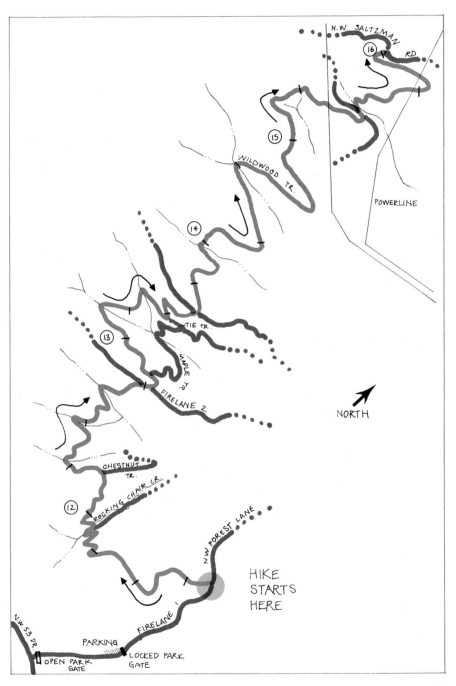

N.W. SALTZMAN RD

POWERLINE

NORTH

WILDWOOD TR.

TIE TR.

MAPLE TR.

FIRELANE 2

CHESTNUT TR.

ROCKING CHAIR CR.

N.W. FOREST LANE

HIKE
STARTS
HERE

FIRELANE 1

N.W. 53 DR.

PARKING

OPEN PARK GATE

LOCKED PARK GATE

67

which is marked by a sign. Follow N.W. Forest Lane (Firelane 1) until it meets a locked park gate. At this point, park your car and hike .3 mile to the trailhead.

THE TRAIL BEGINS between Wildwood Mileposts 11 and 11¼ and almost immediately takes the hiker into a mid-aged conifer stand, laden with a characteristic understory of sword fern and Oregon grape. Some of the numbered signs in this area were part of an old, self-guided tour along Nature Trail. Do not confuse them with Wildwood Trail markers.

Two species of Oregon grape grow in Oregon. Cascade Oregon grape (*Berberis nervosa*), a low-growing shrub that thrives in deep or partial shade, is recognizable by its compound leaves with eleven to twenty-one leaflets. This species occurs from lowlands to mid-elevations and is often a dominant associate of Douglas fir; it is abundant throughout Forest Park. Tall Oregon grape (*Berberis aquifolium*) grows up to six feet high and occurs in more open forests and forest margins of the lowlands. It has five to eleven leaflets per leaf and is the state flower of Oregon. This shrub is rare in the park.

Just after Milepost 11¾, the trail crosses Rocking Chair Creek. After this point Wildwood climbs out of the canyon for .5 mile, and immediately beyond the intersection with Chestnut Trail (*see* HikeThirteen), levels off and passes through a scenic stand of older coniferous trees, which provide a good example of vegetative succession. Note that under the towering Douglas firs, younger western hemlock and western red cedar trees and saplings are growing in abundance. These are the trees that eventually will replace the firs and will command the dominant position in the forest.

After a gentle climb, Wildwood Trail crosses Firelane 2 near Milepost 12¾, then drops again via a series of switchbacks into a steep canyon and a small stream. Along this section, large Douglas fir trees have fallen adjacent to the trail. Violent windstorms downed these trees, for Douglas firs have shallow, small root systems, making them especially vulnerable during high winds and dependent upon other nearby trees for support and protection.

Throughout this section of forest are evidences of fire damage. In 1951, a major burn covering over one thousand acres raged through Forest Park and sites farther west on Bonny Slope. Since that time, the city has initiated many preventative measures, including construction of firebreaks, access roads, and water retention sources, to avert future, similar catastrophes.

At 12.8 miles, Wildwood intersects with Maple Trail (*see* Hike Fourteen). Stay left on Wildwood; for the next .6 mile, the trail wanders through an exquisite section of woods, with stately old Douglas firs creating the effect of a hushed cathedral. Look for tracks and signs of deer and coyote along this stretch. A short distance before Milepost 13½, where Wildwood switches back to the left, the tie-trail to Maple Trail heads off downhill. After Milepost 14, the conifers dwindle off and the trees are mostly young red alder; here vegetative succession has been set back as the result of logging and fire.

Wildwood Trail crosses under a powerline at Milepost 15¼ and the open area surrounding this point allows for an expansive view of the park. At Milepost 15½, Wildwood enters a stand of young, even-aged Douglas fir trees that were planted by volunteers to reforest the hillsides after the disastrous fire. Directly after Milepost 16, Wildwood adjoins N.W. Saltzman Road. Because of vandalism and garbage dumping, this portion of Saltzman Road has been closed off to vehicular traffic, although bicycles and horses are allowed. To reach the parking area, turn left on Saltzman and hike 1.05 miles up the road to a locked park gate. Parking is available here.

WILDWOOD TRAIL

HIKE FOUR

N.W. Saltzman Road to
N.W. Springville Road / MILE 16.0-22.5

DISTANCE: 6.5 miles (one way*) (add an additional 1.4 miles total for access to the trail at both ends)
HIKING TIME: 3 to 3½ hours (one way*) (add an additional ¼ hour total for access to the trail at both ends)
ELEVATION GAIN: 150 feet
HIGH POINT: 900 feet
Foot traffic only.
One way trip; requires a vehicle at both ends of this hike.

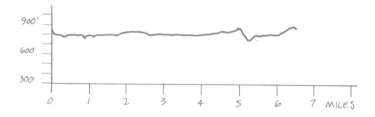

THE PARTICULAR SECTION of trail between N.W. Saltzman (Milepost 16) and Springville roads (Milepost 22½) wanders through remote, little-traveled areas of Forest Park and is enjoyable for its solitude. In the summer this trail is a bower of rural isolation—cooling on a hot day. Introduced plant species such as ivy and holly are rare, while native trees and ground cover thrive, as do naturally occurring mammals and birds of the Northwest, an unusual and exemplary condition for a city park.

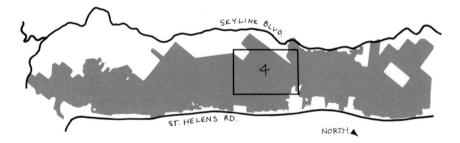

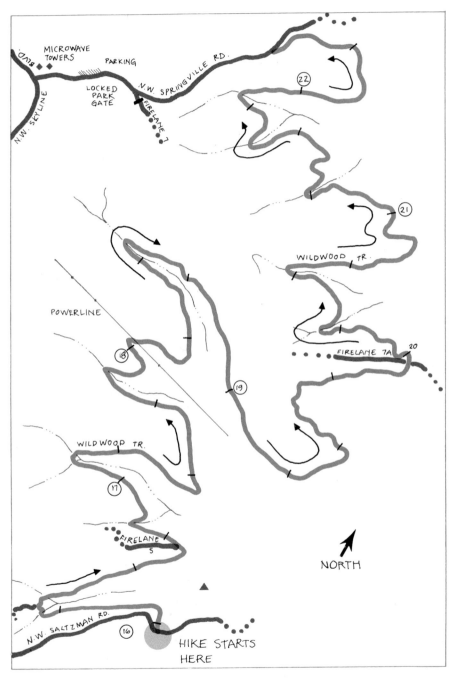

MICROWAVE
TOWERS
PARKING

N.W. SKYLINE BLVD

LOCKED
PARK
GATE

N.W. SPRINGVILLE RD.

FIRELANE 7

22

21

WILDWOOD TR.

POWERLINE

18

FIRELANE 7A

20

19

WILDWOOD TR.

17

FIRELANE 5

NORTH

N.W. SALTZMAN RD.

16

HIKE STARTS
HERE

Access to this part of Wildwood Trail is slightly more difficult than other trails in Forest Park. Both N.W. Saltzman and N.W. Springville roads are closed to through traffic, which means the hiker must walk an additional mile or so at each end of these graveled roads to reach Wildwood Trail.

To begin this hike at the Saltzman Road trailhead, drive west from N.W. 23rd Avenue and N.W. Lovejoy (Lovejoy turns into N.W. Cornell Road after N.W. 25th), traveling 3.3 miles to the junction with N.W. Skyline Boulevard. Turn right onto Skyline and travel 2.9 miles to N.W. Saltzman Road. (To park a car at the end of this hike, drive an additional .9 mile to N.W. Springville Road, to the right just beyond Skyline Milepost 7.) Turn right on Saltzman and continue .15 mile to a locked park gate. Leave the car here (please park on the side so that service vehicles can get through) and proceed on foot down the road for 1.05 miles, where Saltzman Road intersects with Wildwood Trail.

To BEGIN the hike, turn left (north) on Wildwood and descend a rugged canyon to a creek crossing near Milepost 16¼. Here, listen for the call of a pygmy owl, a small, rather tame owl that is active during the day, and gives repetitive single or double coo-like hoots.

For a short distance near Milepost 16½, Wildwood enters a picturesque pocket of mid-aged conifer, then continues farther into an area thick with the growth of young deciduous trees. Fire-scarred stumps and snags of old Douglas fir trees are sprinkled throughout the rapidly growing maples and alders. Beyond Milepost 16½, the trail crosses Firelane 5; continue on Wildwood. From Milepost 16¾ to 17½, numerous side creeks trickle down through the canyon in winter and spring, all heading to the major ravine far below. Past Milepost 17¼, several madrone trees (identifiable by their brown, peeling bark and leathery leaves) occur on southeast-facing slopes. These trees are native to western Oregon, but are usually found in somewhat drier conditions. Through the next several miles, the trail passes under some very large, fallen trees.

Just after Milepost 18, the trail opens into a powerline right-of-way, affording long-distance views of Larch Mountain and Mt. Hood.

Examples of nursery logs are observable near Milepost 18¾. The moist, rotting stumps and downed logs of Douglas fir trees provide essential nutrients for sapling hemlocks, which are often seen growing out of the old fir remnants. Also visible on several large Douglas fir stumps are notches that were chopped decades ago by loggers harvesting the timber. These notches were cut to a specific size so that springboards, usually eight inches wide by five feet long, could be fitted into them. Springboards supported the loggers, who stood on them while they cut the tree down.

Near Milepost 19¼, the evergreen forest canopy opens up again; in winter, when the leaves are off the trees, views of the river and city are outstanding. Swan Island, the University of Portland campus, and the tall towers of downtown Portland are all visible. In spring, when the catkins are out on the deciduous trees, scores of birds flock to feed. Fire signs are evident for the next 1.5 miles, until Milepost 21¼, when the trail crosses a creek overhung by picturesque, older conifers. From this section to the end of this hike, there are several climbs and descents, and the trail crosses some firetrails and grown-over logging roads. At 22.5 miles, Wildwood Trail intersects N.W. Springville Road, deep in the woods and far from traffic and people.

To reach the second car on N.W. Skyline, turn left and hike up Springville .35 mile to the park gate closing the road off to traffic. Skyline is .2 mile beyond this gate.

WILDWOOD TRAIL

N.W. Springville Road to
N.W. Germantown Road / MILE 22.5-24.6

DISTANCE: 2 miles (one way)*
HIKING TIME: 1 hour (one way)
ELEVATION: 800 feet
Foot traffic only.
One way trip; requires a vehicle at both ends of this hike.

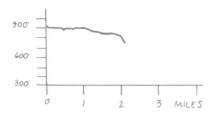

THE SECTION OF TRAIL between Springville (Milepost 22½) and Germantown roads (Milepost 24½) is exceptionally rewarding for its access, easy grade, beautiful stands of old fir trees, and its deep seclusion within the park.

As with all the one-way hikes, this trek can be done from either direction. For continuity with the four preceding hikes, hike north along this trail, beginning at N.W. Springville Road.

To reach this trailhead, drive west from N.W. 23rd Avenue and N.W. Lovejoy, which will become N.W. Cornell Road, traveling 3.3 miles to

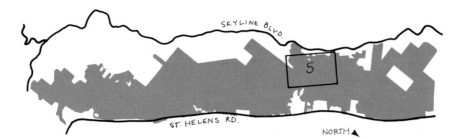

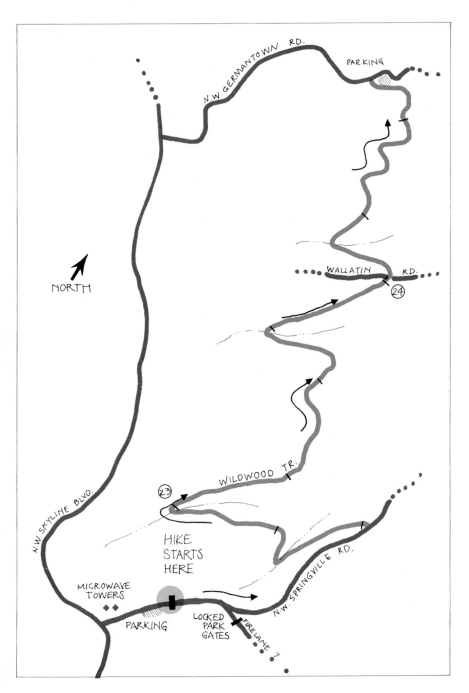

NORTH

N.W. GERMANTOWN RD.

PARKING

WALLATIN RD.

(24)

WILDWOOD TR.

(23)

HIKE
STARTS
HERE

N.W. SKYLINE BLVD.

MICROWAVE
TOWERS

PARKING

LOCKED
PARK
GATES

FIRELANE 7

N.W. SPRINGVILLE RD.

the junction with N.W. Skyline Boulevard. Turn right onto Skyline and travel 3.8 miles to N.W. Springville Road (watch for the microwave tower looming over the trees). Turn right (east) on Springville and drive .2 mile to a locked park gate. Park the car here (making sure not to block access); walk east (passing the locked gate of Firelane 7), and hike the graveled Springville Road .35 mile to the trailhead.

For easier access, do this hike in reverse. Drive 4.7 miles along N.W. Skyline Boulevard to the N.W. Germantown Road junction. Turn east on Germantown Road and drive .5 mile to the trailhead.

THE TRAIL BEGINS at Milepost 22½ with a slight downgrade, which it maintains most of the way from Springville to Germantown Road. Almost immediately, large Douglas firs create a scenic backdrop along the trail, and, in winter, rushing creeks deep in the canyon can be heard. Be sure to note the variety of coniferous trees lining the trail. Tall Douglas firs etch the skyline, while grand fir, western hemlock, and western red cedar grow in the Douglas firs' shade. Someday, if the forest is left alone—and natural vegetative succession is allowed to take place—these younger, more shade-tolerant trees will replace the Douglas firs, and a climax condition will be reached.

For approximately one mile after Milepost 23, the trail winds in and out of exquisite stands of older firs. Indeed, this section may make hikers forget they are only minutes from downtown Portland; here the forest's spell predominates, and the array of native plants and wildlife allow for study and reflection. After Milepost 24½, Wildwood Trail at last comes to its conclusion as it joins N.W. Germantown Road. Space is available here for parking.

WILDWOOD TRAIL

N.W. Germantown Road to
N.W. Newton Street / MILE 24.6-26.3

DISTANCE: 1.7 miles (one way)*
HIKING TIME: One hour (one way)
ELEVATION GAIN: 100 feet
HIGH POINT: 875 feet
Foot traffic only
One way trip; requires a vehicle at both ends of this hike.

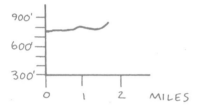

THIS RELATIVELY NEW SECTION of Wildwood Trail captures the peace, solitude and tranquility that symbolizes Forest Park. It is more easily accessible than some sections of Wildwood Trail, and the Germantown Road parking area, where the hike begins, has plenty of room for cars. This hike is a wonderful one to do with children; it is not difficult and gives a good introduction to the wonders of a western Oregon coniferous forest.

To access the trailhead, drive on N.W. Skyline Blvd. until its intersection with N.W. Germantown Road. Turn east (right) on Germantown

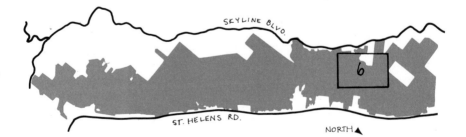

78

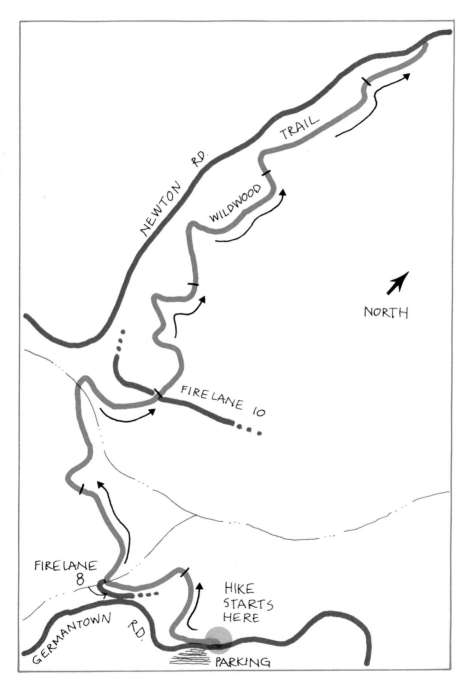

NEWTON RD.

WILDWOOD TRAIL

NORTH

FIRE LANE 10

FIRELANE
8

FIRELANE
8

GERMANTOWN RD.

HIKE
STARTS
HERE

PARKING

79

Road, and continue .5 mile to a large parking area on the right. To begin the hike, cross Germantown Road and access Wildwood Trail, which is denoted by a sign. Head north.

At the beginning of this hike, Wildwood Trail gently winds through forest habitat indicative of the "Western Hemlock Vegetation Zone" of western Oregon and Washington. While walking along, listen closely for the hallmark bird species of this ecosystem: golden crowned kinglets, song sparrows, brown creepers, chestnut-backed chickadees, Steller's jays, red-breasted nuthatches, and winter wrens. All of these native forest birds have easily identifiable songs that are not difficult to learn. The small, brown winter wren exhibits, perhaps, the most amazing song of all. It is high, melodic and clear, and seems to continue on indefinitely, with the tiny bird never pausing for breath. In winter and early spring the winter wren's cheery song may be the only bird heard in the forest.

At Wildwood 25, Firelane 8 comes in to the left; continue on Wildwood and enjoy lovely views of cascading creeks during the rainy seasons of the year. Just past Wildwood 25, the forest character changes for a section. The towering Douglas fir trees give way to a landscape of red alder trees. In spring they transform the forest into a blush of rosy pink. Red alder is known to be beneficial to the soil. Because of its ability to fix atmospheric nitrogen, which increases the nitrogen content and availability in the soil, it can help restore areas where soil nutrients have been depleted, as a result of logging or fire. In addition, red alder leaves break down quickly after they have fallen and provide food for invertebrates that live in the creeks. In turn, these invertebrates provide a food base for fish.

At Wildwood 25.45, Firelane 10 intersects the trail; proceed on Wildwood, and ignore all other side trails coming in. The trail continues to be level and winding. On a fair day, sunlight dapples on the forest floor as it filters though the web of tree branches. Oregon grape, red huckleberry, Indian plum, and other native shrubs carpet the woods. Near Milepost 26, keep a look out for the beautiful, fragrant wild ginger plant growing low to the ground. This forest plant, with its heart-shaped leaves and gingery smell, is especially visible in mid-February—making it a fitting symbol for Valentine's Day—when other shrubs and forbs have not yet leafed out.

Just before the end of the hike, at Milepost 26¼, a few spectacular, old growth Douglas firs grow near the trail and warrant a few minutes observation. The panorama of luxurious growth of trees make it easy to see why the Forest Park Natural Resources Management Plan called Forest Park "the lungs of the City, providing fresh air to the entire region."

At Wildwood 26.3, Newton Street intersects with Wildwood. At this juncture, one can decide whether to back-track 1.7 miles to return to the parking area on N.W. Germantown Road, or turn left (uphill) on Newton Street for .60 mile to another spacious parking area on Newton Street. If one desires only a one-way trip, a second car can be left here.

WILDWOOD TRAIL

N.W. Newton Street to
Firelane 15 / MILE 26.3-28.25

DISTANCE: 1.95 miles (one way)*
HIKING TIME: 1 hour (one way)
ELEVATION GAIN: 225 feet
ELEVATION LOSS: 150 FEET
HIGH POINT: 925 feet
(Note: Wildwood Trail from the Bonneville Powerline Road (Mile 27.45) to Firelane 15 (Mile 28.25) is presently under construction and should be completed by fall of 1996.)
Foot traffic only
One way trip; requires a vehicle at both ends of hike.

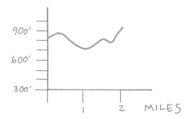

THIS NEWEST SEGMENT of Wildwood Trail takes the hiker into the remote "North Unit" sections of Forest Park, where pedestrians are few and the chance to see native wildlife is enhanced. This part of Forest Park provides important wildlife habitat for many indigenous species. As a hiker walks through these natural areas, the full majesty of Forest Park

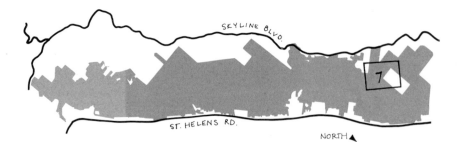

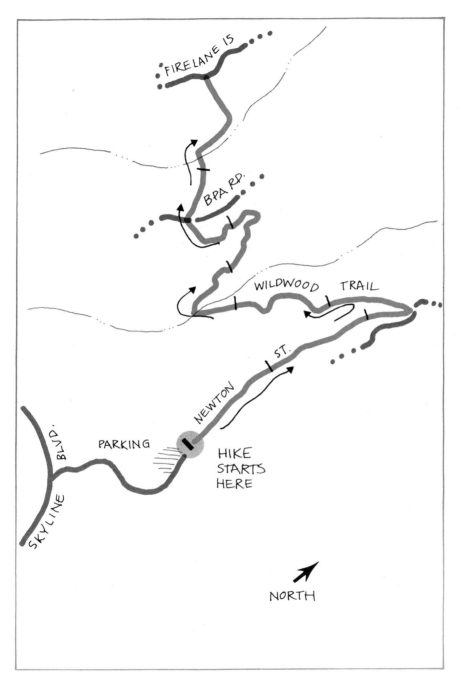

FIRELANE 15

BPA RD.

WILDWOOD   TRAIL

NEWTON   ST.

PARKING

SKYLINE BLVD.

HIKE
STARTS
HERE

NORTH

83

becomes clear, and the words of the 1995 Forest Park Management Plan take on their full meaning: "No other major city in the nation can claim a wilderness-like forest of this magnitude within its boundaries."

To reach the trailhead, drive northwest on N.W. Skyline Blvd. until its intersection with N.W. Newton Street, .5 mile north of N.W. Germantown Road. Turn right (east) on Newton Street and continue down the dirt road for .3 mile, where Newton Street dead ends at a large parking area. Park here, and continue on foot on the continuation of Newton Street—which is accessed at the north end of the parking area, just past a park gate. From this point, Newton Street is closed to all motorized traffic except maintenance vehicles. Wildwood Trail intersects Newton Street after .60 mile. At this juncture, leave Newton Street and turn left (northwest) onto Wildwood Trail.

The section of Wildwood Trail from Newton Street (Mile 26.3) to the Bonneville Powerline Road (Mile 27.45) takes a hiker through quiet, deep woods and provides a fine example of Forest Park's "interior forest habitat." Interior forest habitat is noteworthy for its large, unbroken pieces of native vegetation not dissected by sharp, contrasting areas, such as clearcuts, agricultural fields or residential development. Many species of native mammals and birds are dependent on habitat that occurs deep in the forest, far from the "edge." Animals that frequent forest "edges"— starlings, brown-headed cowbirds, scrub jays, opossums, skunks, among others—often tend to be parasitic or predacious upon forest birds, particularly nesting, migratory songbirds. Throughout the northeastern United States and southeastern coastal plain, for example, regional extinctions have regularly occurred as a result of fragmentation of natural habitat.

Forest Park's interior forest habitat, however, is still predominantly intact in places; it has been deemed, therefore, the park's most unique and valuable asset by the 1995 Forest Park Management Plan. "No other urban park in the United States," states the Plan, "offers anything comparable in quantity and quality."

Near Mile 27.25, Wildwood Trail begins to climb and switchback along an alder ridge. Beautiful vistas open up as the trail approaches the Bonneville Powerline, where an observant hiker might see a red-tailed hawk perching on one of the poles. At Wildwood 27.45, the trail comes out at the Bonneville Powerline Road—a grassy, rock-strewn access road, open only to maintenance vehicles. Turn left on the BPA Road and walk uphill for 100 feet to access the continuation of Wildwood Trail.

This newest portion of the trail winds up and down ravines for three quarters of a mile before reaching Firelane 15. Large western red cedars and delicate vine maples line the trail; prickly salmonberry bushes grow profusely along the creeks. The trail crosses several intermittent tributaries that feed into Miller Creek, a perennial stream that flows from Forest Park into Multnomah Channel. In the entire park, only two streams, Miller and Balch Creeks, are known to contain fish. Like Balch Creek, Miller Creek is *not* open for fishing.

Near Mile 28.25, Wildwood Trail comes out at Firelane 15. At this point, a hiker can choose to walk back on Wildwood Trail to Newton Street, or, if a one-way trip is preferred, to access a second car parked on Skyline Boulevard. For the second option, exit Wildwood Trail at this intersection and walk uphill on Firelane 15 one mile to reach N.W. Skyline Blvd. Limited parking space is available here.

TUNNEL TRAIL
AND TRAILS
SOUTH OF CORNELL ROAD

DISTANCE: 2.5 miles
HIKING TIME: 1 to 1½ hours
ELEVATION GAIN: 420 feet
HIGH POINT: 700 feet
Foot traffic only.

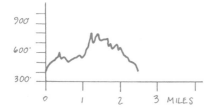

THIS MEDLEY of well-marked, interlinking trails offers an excellent, relatively short hike very close to the city, yet with all the benefits and beauty most often associated with deep, secluded forests. This hike is perfect for an afternoon stroll, relaxing and invigorating to the senses, especially after the fast pace and pressures of city living.

To reach the trailhead, drive through northwest Portland, traveling west from N.W. 23rd on Lovejoy Street (Lovejoy changes to Cornell Road after N.W. 25th) until just past the first tunnel (1.1 miles). At this point there is a pull-out on the left and a trail marker, sometimes hard to see, denoting Tunnel Trail. Park here, and hike south (left) on Tunnel Trail.

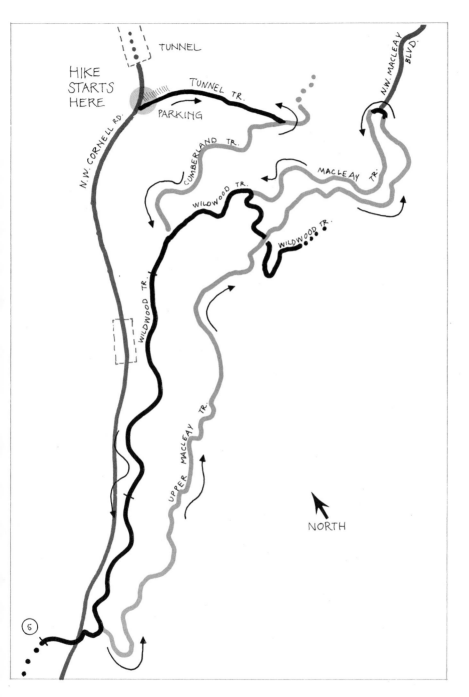

TUNNEL

HIKE
STARTS
HERE

TUNNEL TR.

PARKING

N.W. CORNELL RD.

CUMBERLAND TR.

WILDWOOD TR.

WILDWOOD TR.

WILDWOOD TR.

N.W. MACLEAY BLVD.

MACLEAY TR.

UPPER MACLEAY TR.

NORTH

5

87

THIS SHORT TRAIL (less than .25 mile) is uphill and relatively steep, following a narrow ravine where Douglas firs grow alongside a sonorous creek. In fall, old big leaf maples cast brilliant yellow color, lighting the trail like sunshine. After the first bridge (which is very slippery when wet) the trail has worn down to bedrock, making walking sometimes difficult on a rainy day. But the path soon ends at an intersection with Cumberland Trail. Turn right onto Cumberland Trail and follow the nice, easy grade, contouring in and out of ravines with stands of mid-aged conifer. The trail is wide, well maintained, and lined with native lady and sword ferns.

Non-native, troublesome species such as English holly and ivy are also widespread, escaping from nearby yards and gaining a foothold at the expense of naturally occurring plants. This is the general rule of Forest Park—the closer you are to the city, the greater the percentage of non-native species of vegetation and wildlife. Farther away, at the park's northwest end, these introduced specimens are rare or absent.

After .25 mile, Cumberland Trail reaches a junction with Wildwood Trail. Turn right on Wildwood and follow it .5 mile (passing Mileposts 4½ and 4¾) as it parallels high above Cornell Road. The trail slowly descends and allows some beautiful views of the forested hillside across Cornell Road. In fall, these hills are a patchwork of rich color. Continue on Wildwood as it curves along the sides of ravines, pausing to look at the old snags dotted with woodpecker holes, until the trail comes down almost to road level.

Soon Wildwood Trail junctions with Upper Macleay Trail. Leave Wildwood by turning left on Upper Macleay Trail and continue uphill. For several hundred yards this higher trail parallels Wildwood Trail. Between the tall trees there are views of the Willamette River. The trail levels off and is dotted here and there with huge old Douglas firs, many over one hundred years old, interspersed with old maple trees, sporting green licorice fern growing out of their trunks.

Upper Macleay Trail crosses Wildwood again; continue on Upper Macleay Trail. (Wildwood Trail leads to the right, up to the Pittock Mansion.) Upper Macleay Trail is now far from the road and from here until its end, emanates a peaceful feeling as it gently wanders up and down, crossing wide ravines. Eventually it ends, rather abruptly coming out at a parking area on N.W. Macleay Boulevard in Westover Heights. At the trail's end, make a sharp, left turn onto Macleay Trail, which slopes downhill at a slight grade through beautiful, sun-filtering woods. After .25 mile, Macleay Trail ends, intersecting with Wildwood Trail. Stay to the right, traveling downhill on Wildwood Trail.

Several hundred yards farther, Wildwood again intersects Cumberland Trail. Turn right, heading downhill on Cumberland. At Cumberland's junction with Tunnel Trail, turn left on Tunnel, and follow the steep trail down to Cornell Road and the end of the hike.

ASPEN TRAIL–
HOLMAN LANE LOOP

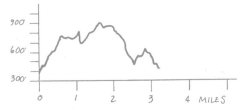

DISTANCE: 3 miles
HIKING TIME: 1½ hours
ELEVATION GAIN: 520 feet
HIGH POINT: 820 feet
Foot traffic only, except for Holman Lane,
which allows bicycles going uphill only.

THIS SHORT, three-mile loop offers a taste of wild Northwest areas and examples of native plants and animals, all within a ten-minute drive from the city.

From downtown Portland, drive west along N.W. Thurman Street from N.W. 23rd (over the Thurman Street bridge) for 1.3 miles to N.W. Aspen Avenue. Turn hard left onto Aspen Avenue, and travel .4 mile to the trailhead, marked with a large wooden sign on the right side of the road.

BEGIN THE HIKE by following Aspen Trail (a short, .22-mile trail) up a steep, ivy-strewn hillside. Once again, ivy makes its appearance in Forest

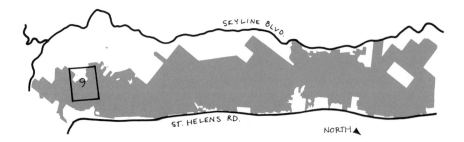

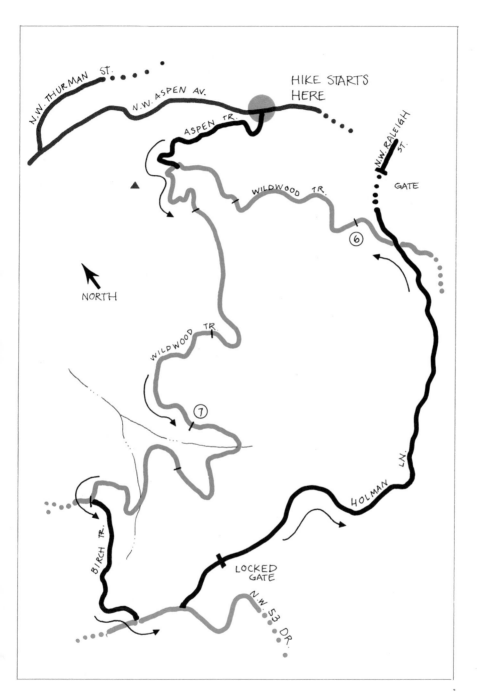

HIKE STARTS
HERE

N.W. THURMAN ST.

N.W. ASPEN AV.

ASPEN TR.

N.W. RALEIGH ST.

GATE

WILDWOOD TR.

⑥

NORTH

WILDWOOD TR.

⑦

HOLMAN LN.

BIRCH TR.

LOCKED
GATE

N.W. 53 DR.

Park in areas close to human habitation; ivy is a nuisance as well as a serious detriment to the native plants. Fortunately, along this trail individuals have girdled the ivy around the trees, which, if done repeatedly, is an effective way to curtail its rapid growth, and free the old conifers and maples from eventual strangulation.

Aspen Trail joins Wildwood Trail prior to Wildwood Milepost 6¼. At the junction, turn right onto Wildwood. In spring trilliums peek out throughout this section of woods. At other times of the year, try to identify the characteristic native plants of western Oregon—Indian plum, sword fern, Oregon grape, red huckleberry, and waterleaf, noting also that now, deeper in the woods, the ivy has dwindled. This portion of Wildwood Trail switchbacks up several hundred feet (passing Milepost 6½) and winds around numerous ravines.

A little more than one mile into this hike (between Mileposts 7 and 7¼) there will be a bridge crossing. Just before Milepost 7½ (twenty-five yards ahead along the trail), Wildwood Trail intersects with Birch Trail (coming in from above and to the left). Turn left onto Birch Trail at this junction. Travel .21 mile on a lightly graveled trail up the canyon, through an area dominated by two deciduous tree species—red alder and big leaf maple.

Birch Trail ends at its intersection with N.W. 53rd Drive; here there are grassy, open meadows on both sides of the street, perfect for relaxing and picnicking in the sun. Picnic tables are provided across N.W. 53rd Drive.

To make the return trip, turn left and hike down N.W. 53rd Drive approximately two hundred yards to an unmarked, gravel road. Turn left onto the road and hike .06 mile to a locked park gate. Continue past this gate along the road, which soon turns into a grassy lane. After another .1 mile, there will be a sign marking Holman Lane, which is a public right-of-way. This open trail provides an excellent opportunity to view bird species characteristic of early successional stage areas—Bewick's wrens, rufous-sided towhees, and white-crowned sparrows, among others. This wide pathway descends the canyon for about .75 mile, allowing expansive views of Macleay Park, Balch Creek Canyon, Cornell Road (across the canyon), the Willamette River, and the Fremont Bridge.

Holman Lane joins Wildwood Trail just before Milepost 6. Below and to the right is a popular picnic area. (Holman Lane extends directly down the hill several hundred yards to the gate at the Raleigh Street entrance to Forest Park.) Turn left onto Wildwood Trail and continue for .43 mile, where Wildwood is joined by Aspen Trail. Turn right on Aspen to descend to the start of this loop. There is a park bench at the trail's end, perfect for quiet contemplation of the completed hike, or for changing out of muddy hiking shoes.

LOWER MACLEAY TRAIL

DISTANCE: 1.4 miles (one way)*
HIKING TIME: ¾ hours (one way)
ELEVATION GAIN: 250 feet
HIGH POINT: 400 feet
Foot traffic only.
One way trip; requires a vehicle at both ends of this hike.

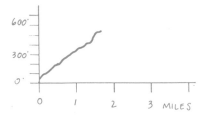

ONE OF THE MOST scenic trails in Forest Park, Lower Macleay Trail is a
magnificent introduction to all the natural and special beauty of the park.
It boasts rushing streams and giant primordial trees, and is easily accessible to persons traveling by car or bus.

On 20 June 1887, Donald Macleay, banker and civic leader, donated
107 acres of land to the city of Portland for a park. The park was called
Macleay Park, and today still retains the same name, though it has been
incorporated into Forest Park.

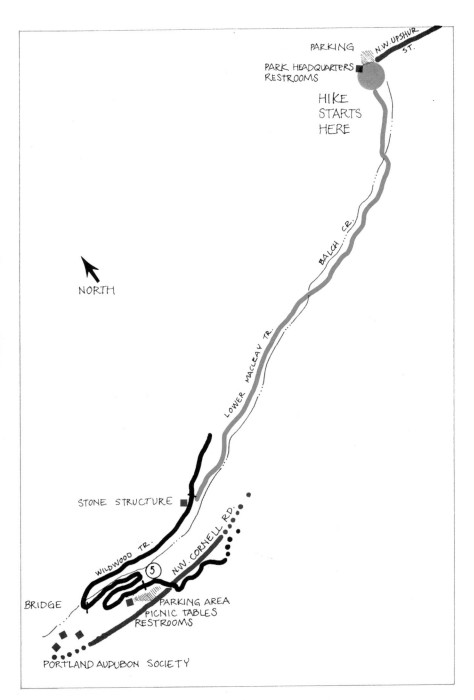

PARKING

N.W. UPSHUR ST.

PARK HEADQUARTERS
RESTROOMS

HIKE
STARTS
HERE

BALCH CR.

NORTH

LOWER MACLEAY TR.

STONE STRUCTURE

NW CORNELL RD.

WILDWOOD TR.

⑤

BRIDGE

PARKING AREA
PICNIC TABLES
RESTROOMS

PORTLAND AUDUBON SOCIETY

To reach the trail by car, drive from N.W. 23rd Avenue on N.W. Thurman Street to N.W. 28th Avenue. Turn right on 28th, then left on N.W. Upshur Street. Continue straight on Upshur (crossing 29th at the stop sign) until it ends at the Lower Macleay Park headquarters. There usually is enough parking in the lot, and on clear days the truncated summit of Mt. St. Helens can be seen from here. There are several picnic tables and restrooms at the trailhead, as well as a wooden jungle gym under the Thurman Street bridge.

Lower Macleay Trail lies exclusively in Balch Creek Canyon. The trail follows Balch Creek, one of few year-round streams flowing in Forest Park. In winter, Balch Creek is a surging stream, home to American Dippers, rapids-loving birds exhibiting the unusual habit of standing underwater!

START THE HIKE along a paved path that passes under the Thurman Street bridge. After 1.5 miles, a footbridge crosses Balch Creek from the north side. Note the profuse growth of maidenhair fern, Douglas fir, and western red cedar. As the trail continues along the south side of the creek, the walls of the canyon become steeper and the stream flow more rapid.

After a short distance, the trail crosses two more bridges; when the stream is full—winter and early spring—the island joined by the two bridges is fully surrounded by the creek's raging water. Here the trail is lined with large fir trees, and the area is filled with the hallmarks of an older coniferous forest—snags, downed logs across the creek, and huge individual trees, including some old-growth specimens.

Stay on Lower Macleay Trail .83 miles, until it comes to a well-marked junction with Wildwood Trail at Milepost 5½. A large, unusual stone structure marks this point. At one time, it was a restroom, complete with running water, until it was heavily vandalized. Lower Macleay Trail ends here.

Continue straight upstream on Wildwood Trail, following it as it parallels Balch Creek. Lovely old-growth trees adorn the trail and outcroppings of Columbia River basalt decorate the creek walls.

After crossing another footbridge at Milepost 5¼, the trail leaves Balch Creek and immediately begins to gain elevation as it switchbacks up to Cornell Road. Wildwood Trail intersects Cornell Road near Milepost 5 (located at a parking area). Just off the trail is a meadow and picnic area with tables and restrooms, providing a place to stop and rest. The Portland Audubon Society headquarters is only several hundred yards to the west of this spot, and a visit to its nature center, excellent bookstore, and adjoining wildlife sanctuaries is well worth the time.

WILD CHERRY–
WILDWOOD–
DOGWOOD TRAIL LOOP

DISTANCE: 1.5 miles
HIKING TIME: ¾ to 1¼ hours
ELEVATION GAIN: 150 feet
HIGH POINT: 900 feet
Foot traffic only.

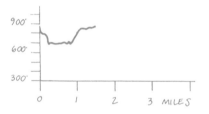

FOR AN EASILY ACCESSIBLE, short walk, the Wild Cherry–Dogwood Loop is one of the nicest in Forest Park. Young children might find this trip an excellent introduction to the joys of hiking. This trail is surrounded by quiet woods, which at times open to reveal splendid views.

To reach the trailhead, drive from N.W. 23rd along N.W. Lovejoy Street, which becomes N.W. Cornell Road after N.W. 25th, traveling for 2.2 miles. Then turn right on N.W. 53rd Drive for .9 miles. At this point there is a large parking area on the right. The entrance to Wild Cherry Trail, which is marked with a sign, is just beyond a park gate.

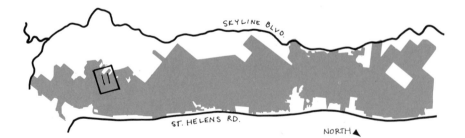

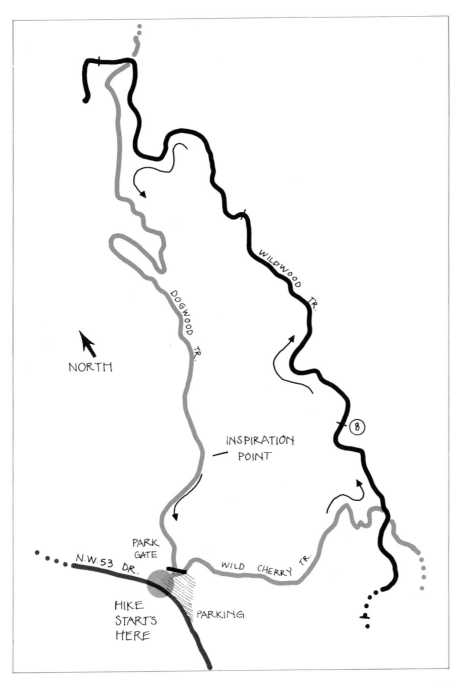

NORTH

WILDWOOD TR.

DOGWOOD TR.

(8)

INSPIRATION
— POINT

PARK
GATE

N.W. 53 DR.

WILD CHERRY TR.

PARKING

HIKE
STARTS
HERE

99

FOLLOW WILD CHERRY TRAIL down a slight grade, which gets progressively steeper with switchbacks to the right and left. About .09 mile into this hike there is a downed tree, which provides a place to sit and enjoy the beauties of Forest Park. The trees along the trail are mostly deciduous (red alder and big leaf maple). Because of the seasonally leafless condition, the ground is exposed in winter and the trail is likely to be muddy.

Wild Cherry intersects with Wildwood Trail after .31 mile. For the loop trip, do not continue on Wild Cherry Trail past this point. Instead, turn left onto Wildwood Trail. This portion of Wildwood, between Mileposts 7¾ and 8¼, is mostly level, winding its way along ravine slopes at a 750-foot elevation. There are several bridges along this section, which can be quite muddy after a rain. Here, many cottonwood trees, which require more water, grow along the side of the trail.

Just before Milepost 8½, Wildwood Trail intersects with Dogwood Trail. Leave Wildwood Trail here and turn left onto Dogwood, following the narrow trail as it winds up several relatively steep switchbacks for .5 mile. Near the top of the ridge, the trail levels off and a lovely stand of coniferous trees borders the trail. The trail was named for the wild dogwood trees that grow along this level section of the trail.

At the crest of Dogwood Trail, an open vista known as Inspiration Point looks out over a panoramic scene of the Willamette River and the city of Portland. When foliage is full, as in spring and early summer, the vista is narrowed. Unfortunately, this popular spot has been much abused and the vegetation almost denuded; often it is littered with fire remains and broken bottles. The site speaks loudly of the problem that plagues spots in Forest Park—unlawful dumping of garbage, a worrisome concern to all who care about the natural beauty of the park.

To finish the loop, continue on the final leg of Dogwood Trail as it leads downhill, passing a small open meadow on the right, dotted in spring with daffodils escaped from home gardens. Dogwood Trail ends back at the parking area on N.W. 53rd Drive.

WILDWOOD– DOGWOOD– ALDER TRAIL LOOP

DISTANCE: 2.65 miles
HIKING TIME: 1½ to 2¼ hours
ELEVATION GAIN: 375 feet
HIGH POINT: 825 feet
Foot traffic only.

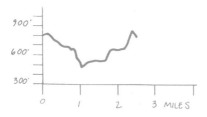

THE ABUNDANCE of deciduous trees along this close-in hike allows views of the Willamette River in winter, and in summer, a respite of cool, leafy shadiness on a hot day. The open sections of this trail provide a chance to observe a wild black-tailed deer or a rare goldback fern–ample rewards for this short, easy loop trip.

To reach the trailhead, follow N.W. Lovejoy Street from N.W. 23rd (Lovejoy will become N.W. Cornell Road) past two tunnels and over three bridges, and past the Portland Audubon Society buildings on the right, a total of 2.2 miles. Turn right on N.W. 53rd Drive (it is easy to miss this turnoff), and follow this road uphill for 1.1 miles. There is a parking

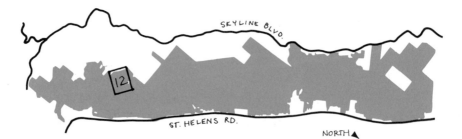

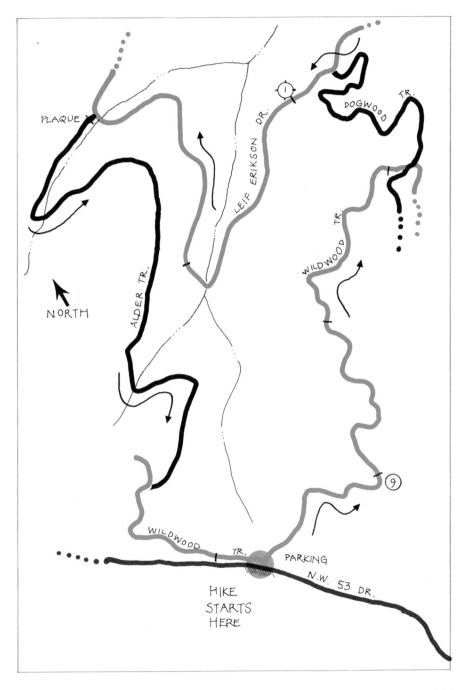

PLAQUE

DOGWOOD TR.

LEIF ERIKSON DR.

WILDWOOD TR.

ALDER TR.

NORTH

1

9

WILDWOOD TR.

PARKING

N.W. 53 DR.

HIKE
STARTS
HERE

area on the right (with signs for Wild Cherry and Dogwood trails), but continue past it for another .1 mile to reach the entrance to this trail (there will be signs to the trail on the right). There are small pullouts on both sides of the road for parking.

BEGIN THE HIKE by turning right on Wildwood Trail and heading southeast, past Milepost 9. This section of trail is relatively level, curving in and out of ravines, and is lined with red alder, big leaf maple, and large Douglas fir trees. Soon after passing Milepost 8½, Dogwood Trail intersects Wildwood. Turn left on Dogwood, and as the trail descends steeply, note that between the trees views of the Willamette River and the north portion of the city of Portland are visible. The careful observer might also spy blue elderberry shrubs and Pacific yew trees, both uncommon in Forest Park.

Continue .33 mile on Dogwood. After passing over a footbridge, Dogwood Trail meets Leif Erikson Drive, an open, wide expanse of road with splendid views of the ravine on the right. Turn left and follow Leif Erikson .57 mile. At many locations along the road, look for well-defined outcroppings of Columbia River basalt. Several species of plants thrive in the cracks of the rock, notably licorice fern, sword fern, and, more rarely, goldback fern, a delicate plant which can be identified by its small triangular fronds, green above but with spores resembling flecks of gold underneath.

At Leif Erikson Milepost 1½, Alder Trail, marked by a large plaque, comes in from above and to the left. Turn left on Alder and follow it as it ascends the canyon. The trail (which can be quite overgrown in the spring and early summer, and muddy on the lower reaches after a rain) is well named, for the predominant trees are deciduous—red alder and big leaf maple. These two species are easily differentiated, even in winter, by their bark. Trunks of big leaf maple have long, vertical furrows in their bark, whereas red alder bark is smooth and gray, with horizontal markings, and is usually covered with lichens.

After .84 mile, Alder Trail joins again with Wildwood. The last few hundred yards are steep. Turn left on Wildwood Trail and continue .22 mile to the end of the hike.

WILDWOOD–
CHESTNUT–
NATURE TRAIL LOOP

DISTANCE: 2.5 miles
HIKING TIME: 1¼ to 2 hours
ELEVATION GAIN: 400 feet
HIGH POINT: 950 feet
Foot traffic only.

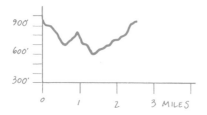

THIS EXTREMELY PLEASANT TRAIL offers solitude, beauty, and natural history features of educational value in a relatively gentle terrain–all within a short drive from town.

To reach the trailhead, drive from N.W. 23rd along N.W. Lovejoy Street, which becomes N.W. Cornell Road after N.W. 25th, traveling 2.2 miles, then turn right on N.W. 53rd Drive for 1.7 miles. Turn right again on Forest Lane (Firelane 1), which is marked by a sign; continue until it meets a park gate. This gate is always locked. Park here and continue on foot along Firelane 1 for .3 mile until it reaches the trailhead.

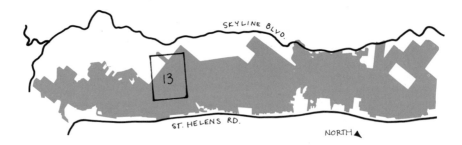

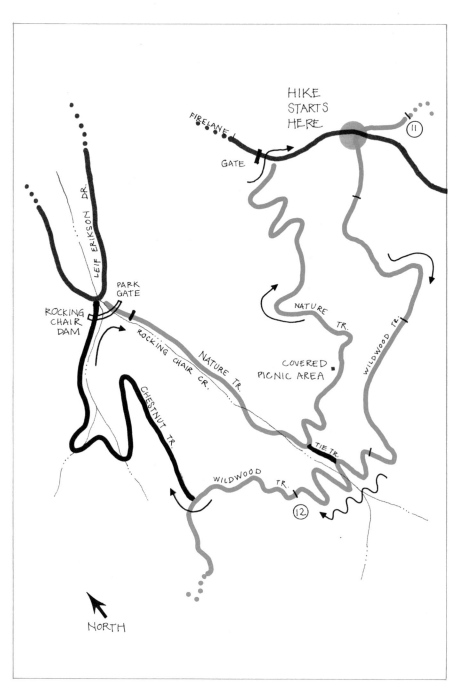

HIKE
STARTS
HERE

FIRELANE I

GATE

LEIF ERIKSON DR.

PARK GATE

ROCKING CHAIR DAM

ROCKING CHAIR CR.

NATURE TR.

CHESTNUT TR.

NATURE TR.

COVERED PICNIC AREA

WILDWOOD TR.

WILDWOOD TR.

TIE TR.

NORTH

To start this hike, turn left on Wildwood (Milepost 11¼); the trail leads north and gently descends into a forested canyon. Notice the pistol-butted Douglas firs—trees in which the lower part of the trunk is curved like a pistol grip. This phenomenon is the result of earth slides that occurred when the trees were young, forcing the trees to angle downhill. In an effort to reach out for sunlight, the trees compensated by growing upward. Pistol-butted trees are commonly observed throughout steep, moist ravines in the Douglas fir forests of western Oregon.

A side trail coming in from the right adjoins Wildwood beyond Milepost 11¾. This is the tie-trail to Nature Trail. For a shorter hike, leave Wildwood at this point and proceed right on the tie-trail, then right again on Nature Trail, which loops back one mile to the parking area.

To continue on the main loop, stay on Wildwood. At the bottom of the ravine, cross Rocking Chair Creek, named long ago for a lone rocking chair discovered sitting on the stream bottom. The trail continues uphill .5 mile. Past Milepost 12, Chestnut Trail joins Wildwood from the right. Turn right on Chestnut Trail and descend a narrowing canyon via several switchbacks for .5 mile, paralleling in parts an exceptionally pretty creek. The trail comes out on Leif Erikson Drive near a large horse chestnut tree. This introduced species is the namesake of Chestnut Trail.

At this junction, turn right onto Leif Erikson Drive for a few hundred feet, and then right again onto Nature Trail, closed off to vehicular travel by a gate. Here is Rocking Chair Dam, a small drainage retention structure at the bottom of Rocking Chair Creek. The often muddy, grass-covered sediment behind the dam is an excellent place to look for tracks, especially those of raccoon, black-tailed deer, and possibly, coyote.

Continue on Nature Trail one mile, crossing two footbridges. Along the trail are several numbered markers, which were keyed to an environmental educational handbook used at one time by Portland Public Schools and the Park Bureau. Halfway up the trail is a sheltered picnic area with several tables and a restroom, all donated by the North Portland Kiwanis and constructed by the Neighborhood Youth Corps.

Nature Trail comes out in an open, grassy meadow just below the parking area on Firelane 1. This green meadow is a perfect place to relax and enjoy the warming sunshine after a rejuvenating forest hike.

MAPLE TRAIL

DISTANCE: 7.25 miles round trip. (Can be broken up into smaller trips)
HIKING TIME: 3½ hours
ELEVATION GAIN: 400 feet
HIGH POINT: 870 feet
Foot traffic only.

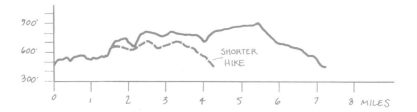

MAPLE TRAIL is one of the most scenic in Forest Park. In fall, its abundance of big leaf maples shimmer with colorful highlights against the dark green of the tall firs. This quiet, woodland hike, deep in the heart of the park, offers remoteness and quiet, and the chance to hear the wild cry of a pileated woodpecker, or to see the fleeting form of a black-tailed deer.

To reach the trailhead, drive on St. Helens Road (U.S. Hwy. 30) 3.2 miles from the intersection of N.W. 23rd Avenue and N.W. Vaughn Street to N.W. Saltzman Road. Watch for Department of Environmental Quali-

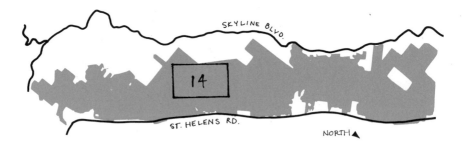

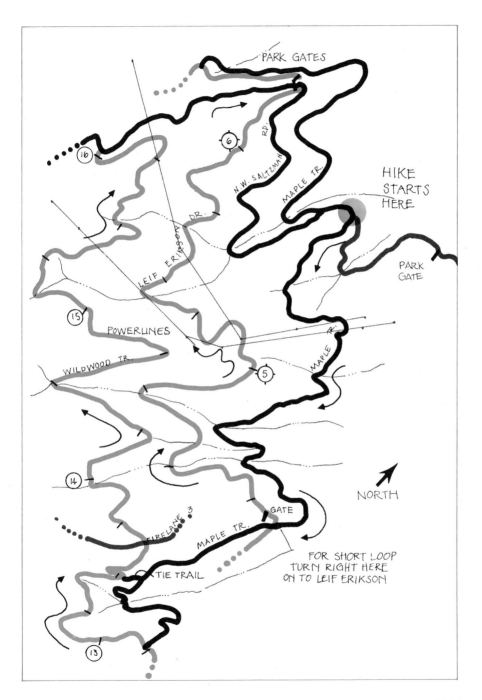

PARK GATES

HIKE STARTS HERE

PARK GATE

16

6

RD.

N.W. SALTZMAN

MAPLE TR.

LEIF ERIKSON DR.

15

POWERLINES

WILDWOOD TR.

5

MAPLE TR.

14

NORTH

FIRELANE 3

GATE

MAPLE TR.

TIE TRAIL

FOR SHORT LOOP
TURN RIGHT HERE
ON TO LEIF ERIKSON

13

ty (DEQ) signs, because Saltzman is located adjacent to the DEQ building's parking lot. Turn left onto Saltzman and drive the paved, winding road .7 mile until reaching a park gate. The gate may or may not be locked. If it is, park the car here and walk an additional .5 mile up the road to a wide turnout near the trailhead. Here there will be two trail markers (which can be difficult to see if grasses are high), both indicating Maple Trail, one pointing right (north) and one left (south). Take the left (south) trail.

AT THE START of the hike, Maple Trail gradually heads uphill among old, big leaf maples and profusely growing alder. Some tall, ninety-year-old Douglas firs grow in isolated spots and tower above the maple and alder. In the understory, look for grand fir and western hemlock trees. These trees will replace the maples within the next one hundred years.

The trail winds along .25 mile, reaching a relatively open, flat area dominated by maple trees and a low-growing, sword fern understory. It then turns upward, and after another .25 mile comes out onto an open, transmission line crossing. At this junction are several shrubs of red flowering currant, planted by volunteers in years past. In spring, their bright blooms attract Anna's and Rufous hummingbirds. On the left, an unpaved, utilities access road is visible. For a short side trip, follow it .08 mile up a relatively steep hill. Here is a panoramic view of the Willamette and Columbia rivers, mountain peaks, bridges, the city, and industrial areas. Deer like this open area, evidenced by their tracks often left in the mud at the hilltop.

Return to Maple Trail by first crossing under the powerlines. This strip of grass-forb and shrub successional stages beneath the towers attracts early successional bird species in the spring, and it is worth pausing for a moment to pick out the wildlife rarely seen deep in the forest. Watch for red-tailed hawks, which like to sit on top of the power poles while they scan the hillside for prey.

Continue on Maple Trail, passing through beautiful patches of vine maple and by isolated madrone trees. At .75 mile, the trail drops down into a ravine of cedar and hemlock, strewn with low-growing Oregon oxalis plants. After crossing a picturesque footbridge, look for maidenhair fern growing beside the trail. After crossing an intermittent stream, the path winds out of the first ravine, turns right, and then back into a second narrow, cedar- and hemlock-covered ravine. A small trail joins Maple from the right at 1.08 mile, but stay on Maple Trail. Cross a second bridge at 1.12 miles; continue on, and the Willamette River again becomes visible.

Eventually the cedars and hemlocks blend into maples, with a sword fern and red-elderberry understory covering a flatter, open area. The trail comes out onto Leif Erikson Drive near Leif Erikson Milepost 4¼.

FOR A SHORTER, 4.25-mile trip, turn right on Leif Erikson and continue walking the wide, well-graded, gravel road for two miles. At Leif Erikson Milepost 4¾, be sure to notice the Columbia River basalt outcropping, with tangles of licorice fern growing in decaying pockets. Just before Milepost 6¼, Leif Erikson Drive intersects with Saltzman Road. Turn right and proceed .75 mile down Saltzman Road to the trailhead.

TO MAKE the longer loop, cross Leif Erikson Drive and continue up the hill on Maple Trail, marked with a sign (note the gate to the right on Firelane 3). For .34 mile, the trail climbs slightly and then intersects with a tie-trail to Wildwood Trail. Continue straight on Maple Trail, descending over a bridge and down three switchbacks to a creek bottom where there are examples of lacy, green maidenhair fern. The trail then climbs out of the canyon and joins again with Wildwood Trail (between Wildwood Mileposts 12¾ and 13). At this junction, turn right onto Wildwood, and hike north for three miles. In early spring, notice the scores of trilliums that line the trail.

Near Wildwood Milepost 16, the trail dips down to Saltzman Road. At this intersection, leave Wildwood and turn right onto the road. Hike down Saltzman for approximately .5 mile to the intersection of Saltzman Road and Leif Erikson Drive.

Turn left onto Leif Erikson Drive. There will be a concrete post denoting 6¼ miles. Continue north on Leif Erikson for .25 mile, and, at the first left turn on Leif Erikson Drive, look for a sign denoting Maple Trail in a clearing to the right.

At this point, leave Leif Erikson Drive and rejoin Maple Trail. This mile-long section of trail wanders in and out of quiet, deep woods – crossing footbridges surrounded by verdant waterleaf plants and ferns, and overhung by western hemlock trees. The trail climbs slightly at the end and comes out at the trailhead, completing the loop.

FIRELANES 15, 12– BONNEVILLE POWERLINE ROAD LOOP

DISTANCE: 3.25 miles
HIKING TIME: 1¾ to 2½ hours
ELEVATION GAIN: 467 feet
HIGH POINT: 1,067 feet
Foot traffic only.

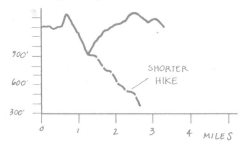

THESE LITTLE-TRAVELED, northernmost trails in Forest Park provide the best chance to see wildlife rarely observed near a major city. Their distance from the city and from population concentrations allow native creatures–black-tailed deer, coyote, red-tailed hawks, and pileated woodpeckers–the opportunity to traverse more freely and openly, and greatly rewards the quiet, patient observer who spies them.

In this area, it is easy to observe the corridor of forest that connects Portland's great urban park with the Coast Range. This corridor, presently free from urbanization, is the primary reason for Forest Park's great wildlife diversity. It allows easy access of native birds and mammals from

114

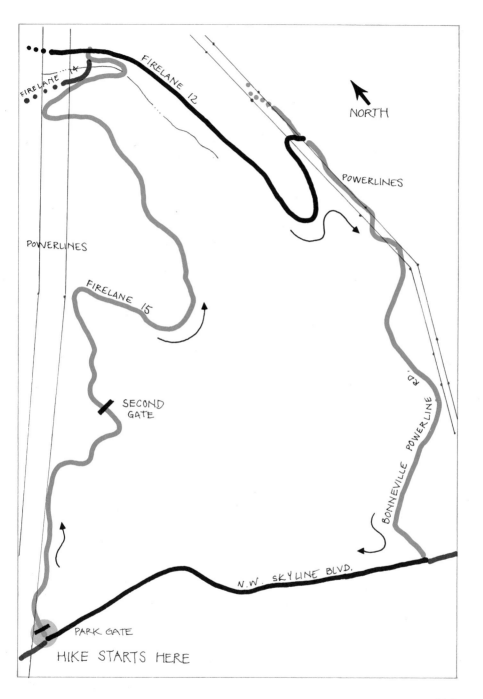

NORTH

FIRELANE 14

FIRELANE 12

POWERLINES

POWERLINES

FIRELANE 15

SECOND GATE

BONNEVILLE POWERLINE RD.

N.W. SKYLINE BLVD.

PARK GATE

HIKE STARTS HERE

other native species pools into Forest Park. In fact, the future capacity of Forest Park to support wildlife will largely be determined by the park's boundary conditions. If this corridor of natural habitat is cut off from Forest Park, making the park an island surrounded on all sides by urban growth, the capability of the park to sustain a diversity of wildlife and plant species will be dramatically reduced.

At the present time, some of this area (near Firelane 15) lies adjacent to private holdings. Several large parcels within the designated Forest Park boundary have yet to be acquired. Land purchase by the city has been slow, and today private holdings can pose a threat to the integrity and original vision of Forest Park. Some of the hikes come close to private property, so please stay on the trails.

To reach the trailhead, drive west from N.W. 23rd along N.W. Lovejoy Street to where it becomes N.W. Cornell Road, continuing 3.3 miles until its intersection with N.W. Skyline Boulevard. Turn right on N.W. Skyline and follow it 6.3 miles to Firelane 15 (two major transmission lines pass over Skyline at this point). The graveled entrance to Firelane 15 can be recognized by the park gate on the right side of the road.

PARK THE CAR, and begin hiking the firelane as it drops down, levels off, drops again, then climbs through a variety of second- and third-growth fir trees. At several spots, Firelane 15 opens to panoramic views of the Columbia River, Sauvie Island, Mt. Rainier, Mt. St. Helens, and the corridor of forestland (mentioned above) connecting Forest Park's northwestern boundary with the rural habitat of the Coast Range.

Stay on Firelane 15 past a second gate, and continue along the gravel road for .6 mile. Portions of the trail beyond this point can be quite muddy after a substantial rain. The trail descends and enters stands of large second-growth conifers (mid-aged conifer successional stage), where signs of woodpecker holes are evident on stumps and snags. At the bottom of the canyon, approximately 1.25 miles from the start of the hike, there is a small creek crossing and an intersection of three trails—Firelanes 15, 14, and 12, marked by a sign.

FOR A SHORTER, gentle hike along an alder-strewn pathway, continue down the canyon on Firelane 12, parallel to the creek, for 1.25 miles. This is a one-way trip, and requires a vehicle at both ends of the hike.

FOR THE LOOP TRIP back to the car, make a right turn at the three-firelane intersection and hike up the canyon on Firelane 12. Climb out of the canyon along Fireland 12's relatively steep incline. At the top, Firelane 12 joins Bonneville Powerline Road. Turn right on Bonneville Powerline Road. This ridge-top trail, which parallels overhead Bonneville Power Administration (BPA) powerlines, is a good place to scan for tracks and scat of black-tailed deer, bobcats, coyotes, and to spot red-tailed hawks, which often perch on top of the power poles. Scenic views of Mt. St. Helens and Mt. Rainier are visible.

After another .7 mile, Bonneville Powerline Road ends at its junction with N.W. Skyline Boulevard. To reach the original starting point, turn right on Skyline and walk west on the road for a final .5 mile.

TRILLIUM TRAIL– WILDWOOD TRAIL– GAS LINE ROAD/ FIRELANE 7 LOOP

DISTANCE: 2.80 miles
HIKING TIME: 1½ to 2½ hours
ELEVATION GAIN: 300 feet
ELEVATION LOSS: 300 feet
HIGH POINT: 1,050 feet
Trillium Trail, Wildwood Trail, foot traffic only. Firelane 7 also open for horses.

THIS LOVELY HIKE is aptly named: in spring these trails abound with beautiful trilliums. But the loop is enjoyable in other seasons as well. In winter, when leaves are off the trees, expansive views of the Willamette River and majestic peaks of the Cascade Range can be seen. In summer, the ever-cool forest provides a welcome respite from the concrete and sweltering heat of the City, while in fall, the colors of the hardwood trees cast streams of yellow against a backdrop of green.

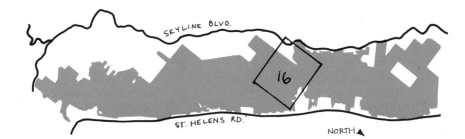

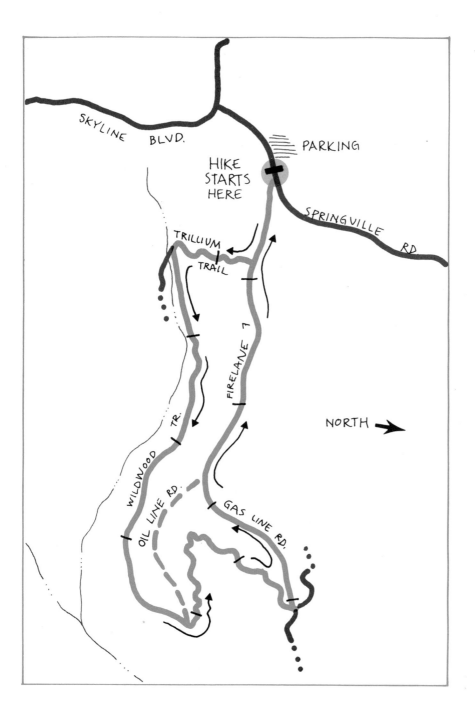

SKYLINE   BLVD.

PARKING

HIKE
STARTS
HERE

SPRINGVILLE
RD.

TRILLIUM
TRAIL

FIRELANE 7

NORTH →

WILDWOOD TR.

OIL LINE RD.

GAS LINE RD.

To reach the trailhead, drive north on N.W. Skyline Blvd. until its intersection with Springville Road. Turn right (east) on Springville, and continue on for .2 mile to the Springville parking area.

Begin the hike by walking around a locked park gate and veer to the right onto Firelane 7. Posts denoting a N.W. Natural Gas line–an eight-inch buried line under pressure–continue at intervals down Firelane 7. To the north, at .13 mile past the park gate, runs the Hardesty Trail. Do not follow this trail, but continue on Firelane 7 about 100 yards further. On the right, at the location of another gas line post, will be the unmarked "Trillium Trail." At this juncture, turn right (south) and begin walking down the narrow and, at spots, fairly steep and sometimes muddy trail.

Red alder and big leaf maple line the hillsides along Trillium Trail for most of its .25 miles. From the trees, listen for the loud, sharp "peeks" of hairy woodpeckers, which prefer this kind of habitat. In late February and early March be on the watch for the first trilliums of spring. These delicately scented flowers sometimes form large patches of closely growing plants, and can create the impression of a carpet of white. The trillium's three, showy petals are at first snowy white. As the flower ages, they will change in color to pink then purple.

After .25 mile, Trillium Trail ends at its intersection with Wildwood Trail. Turn left (north) on Wildwood Trail, and notice that interspersed within the forest of red alder and maple are tall, dead, cedar snags. These snags are silent but telling remnants of a devastating forest fire–sweeping over 1200 acres in three days–that occurred in Forest Park over forty years ago. Since that time, a stringent plan for fire suppression has been enacted and no serious fires have occurred in Forest Park.

Continue on Wildwood Trail for approximately one and a half miles. A host of important berry-producing plants, including serviceberry, madrone, and Oregon grape, can be observed growing on the south facing slopes near Wildwood Milepost 19. In Forest Park, these plants and other berry-producing shrubs (red and blue elderberry, cascara, salmonberry, salal, huckleberry, thimbleberry, and snowberry) are a significant food source for at least thirty-six species of resident and migrant Forest Park birds.

Oil Line Road intersects with Wildwood Trail approximately 300 yards past Wildwood Milepost 19¼. For a shorter loop, take this trail, which connects with Firelane 7, and arrive at the Springville parking area after a gentle but steady uphill climb for one mile. To continue the hike, however, continue on Wildwood Trail for another half-mile to Gas Line Road. Gas Line Road—not a paved road at all, but a grass-strewn, wide pathway—intersects Wildwood Trail just before Wildwood Milepost 20. Exit Wildwood at this point and turn left up Gas Line Road. In winter, when the alder and maple are free of leaves, be sure to look for views of the Willamette River, Mt. St. Helens and Mt. Adams to the northeast. In early summer, watch for beautiful, native tiger lilies growing near the trail. These showy orange lilies, growing from one to eight feet tall, are abundant in Forest Park. As with all native plants, they should never be picked but left to regenerate year after year for everyone's enjoyment.

Continue uphill on Gas Line Road for .33 miles. At this point, Gas Line Road intersects with Firelane 7. Proceed up Firelane 7 for an additional .65 miles, until its end at the Springville Road parking area, which completes the loop.

FIRELANE NINE–
LINNTON–
FIRELANE TEN LOOP

DISTANCE: 2.03 miles
HIKING TIME: 1½ to 2½ hours
ELEVATION LOSS: 550 feet
ELEVATION GAIN: 600 feet
HIGH POINT: 700
Foot traffic only on Firelane 9 and Firelane 10-spur. Firelane 10 is also open to both bicycles and horses.

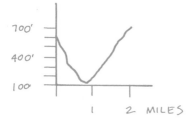

THIS STEEP AND OFTEN MUDDY TRAIL provides a good workout for the hiker wishing more strenuous exercise. Be sure to wear sturdy hiking shoes to give yourself maximum advantage with the hike's elevation gains and losses. This hike affords excellent spots for bird watching, especially in spring with the return of colorful, migrating songbirds. Firelane 10-spur is one of the few trails in Forest Park that can be accessed from St. Helen's Road, the park's eastern boundary. No public parking is available at the turnout on St. Helen's Road, however.

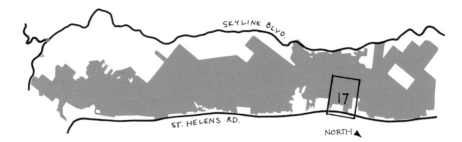

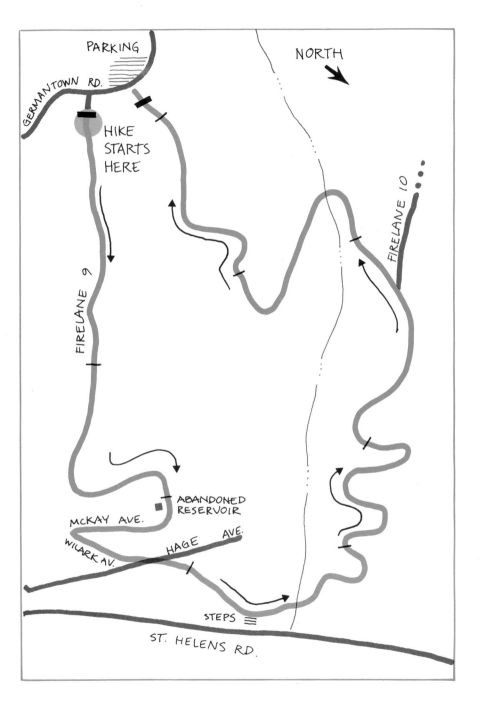

PARKING

NORTH

GERMANTOWN RD.

HIKE STARTS HERE

FIRELANE 9

FIRELANE 10

ABANDONED RESERVOIR

MCKAY AVE.

WILARK AV.

HAGE AVE.

STEPS

ST. HELENS RD.

If coming by car to the trailhead, drive west along N.W. Skyline to the N.W. Germantown Road junction. Turn east on Germantown and drive .5 mile to a large parking area.

To begin the loop, cross Germantown Road and look for a park gate and sign denoting Firelane 9. Walk around the gate and proceed down the steep and sometimes very slippery firelane. Beautiful views of the Willamette River are visible for much of Firelane 9's .64 miles. Red alder and big leaf maple are the predominant trees lining the trail. In spring, when both of these varieties are bearing seeds and catkins, an assortment of brightly colored, songbirds often flock together to feed. Sometimes, in one small cluster of trees, a lucky bird watcher will spy western tanagers, evening grosbeaks, warbling vireos, and several species of warblers all feasting together and creating a cacophony of song.

As Firelane 9 nears St. Helen's Road, the trail begins to level out as it zigzags towards the town of Linnton. An intermittent creek that in winter packs a surprising velocity comes in from above. Several debris catchers are built at intervals along the creek to catch trash and forest debris before it can enter a large culvert that goes under the road. Also visible is the remains of an old, abandoned concrete reservoir, that in the past was used to store water for the town of Linnton.

At its conclusion, Firelane 9 intersects with MacKay Ave. Follow Mac-Kay until it joins N.W. Wilark Ave. At this point, a hiker leaves the park for .3 miles. Turn left on N.W. Wilark, cross Hoge Ave. and continue on Wilark until its end. To the right is a public staircase leading to St. Helen's Highway. Descend the steps and turn left at the bottom, onto a walkway that parallels and is separated from the road. This walkway comes out at the Linnton bus turnout. Continue walking halfway around the turnout, until a trail comes in on the left, just northwest of a sizeable creek.

This trail is presently unmarked and is an offshoot of Firelane 10. It is commonly known as Firelane 10/spur. Further improvements and better signage for this section of the trail are in the planning phases. Begin heading up the trail, leaving St. Helen's Road behind. Along this section of Firelane 10, notice the preponderance of ivy that has choked out most of the native trillium and other native herbaceous plants. A dense cover of ivy such as this can also prevent conifers, notably Douglas fir, from ever reestablishing a site. In doing so, much food and cover is eliminated for many birds, small mammals, and amphibians, which potentially could wreak havoc in native wildlife populations.

Ivy, an exotic, invasive species, can easily escape from residential areas where it is planted for a ground cover. Unfortunately, it has spread into Forest Park wherever residential development borders the park, and is creating serious problems. For these reasons, the Forest Park Natural Resources Management Plan has deemed the removal of ivy the park's highest natural resource management priority. The Plan calls it an "all or nothing proposition," and is concerned that, without very aggressive ivy removal programs, Forest Park could over time potentially be transformed into a "5,000-acre ivy desert."

Continue up Firelane 10/spur which follows the picturesque creek for much of its way. The trail switchbacks as it climbs steadily upward and portions of it can be rough and steep. An alert observer may catch sight of Pacific yew trees growing intermixed with Douglas fir and western hemlock. Pacific yew, a native, evergreen tree well known for its cancer fighting chemical "taxol," is uncommon in Forest Park but identifiable by its soft, reddish-purple bark.

After .4 miles, Firelane 10/spur intersects with Firelane 10. Turn left on Firelane 10, which is a large, wide dirt (and in sections, gravel) road. Sweeping views of deep, forested canyons lushly vegetated with large, old coniferous trees are visible along this trail.

Continue on Firelane 10 for .63 miles. The Firelane ends at its junction with N.W. Germantown Road. Turn left on Germantown Road and walk .06 miles further to reach the parking area and complete the loop.

NEWTON STREET– WILDWOOD TRAIL– FIRELANE 10 LOOP

DISTANCE: 3.95 miles
HIKING TIME: Approximately 2 hours
ELEVATION LOSS: 350 feet
ELEVATION GAIN: 450 feet
HIGH POINT: 875 feet
Foot traffic only on Wildwood Trail. Newton Street and Firelane 10 allow both horses and bicycles.

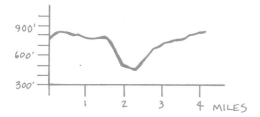

THIS HIKE OFFERS VARIETY. From the rolling terrain of Newton Street, the steep but beautiful downgrade and upgrade of Firelane 10, and the tranquil beauty of Wildwood Trail, this loop is both a workout and a forest respite. It is also easily accessible from Skyline Blvd. and has plenty of parking available.

The trail begins at the large parking area on Newton Street. To reach Newton Street, drive northwest along N.W. Skyline Blvd. and cross N.W. Germantown Road. Continue on N.W. Skyline for .5 mile past German-

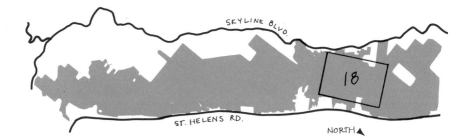

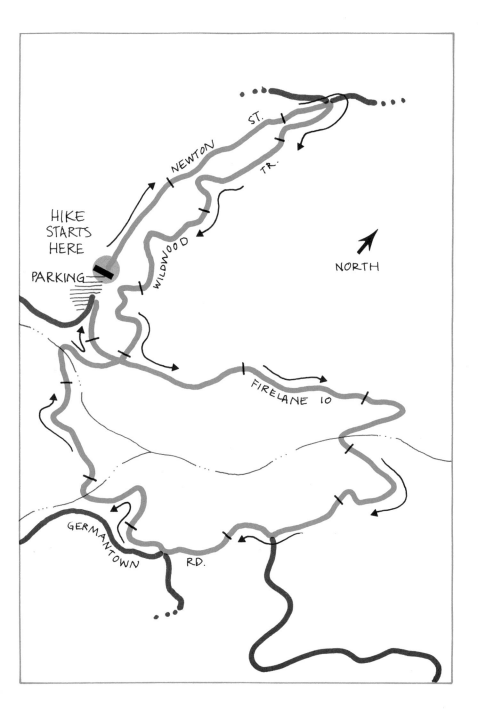

HIKE
STARTS
HERE

PARKING

NEWTON ST.

WILDWOOD TR.

NORTH

FIRELANE 10

GERMANTOWN RD.

127

town. Here, Newton Street takes off to the right. Drive down Newton Street for .3 mile, until it widens out to form a parking area. Vehicular access ends here; the rest of Newton Street is available to foot, horse or bike traffic only.

Begin the loop by walking around a park gate at the north end of the parking area. This wide, grassy trail is the continuation of Newton Street. Initially, the grade is gentle, but soon climbs uphill steeply. After this rise, the trail levels out again for easy walking. Along this section, notice the deep, coniferous forest that stretches to the north of Newton Street. Here, in isolated pockets, majestic old growth trees, giant downed logs, and large snags can be found. All of these features are remnants of the old growth forest that historically covered much of Forest Park.

After .6 mile, Newton Street intersects with Wildwood Trail. At this juncture, turn right onto Wildwood Trail. Continue walking on the level, enjoyable trail (described in Hike Six), for .87 mile, until its intersection with Firelane 10.

Firelane 10, a dirt and gravel road that widens, narrows and widens again at intervals, provides a strenuous hike in spots. Initially the downgrade is very steep, reminiscent of a hike in the Columbia Gorge. Dense, picturesque stands of Douglas fir and western hemlock grow thickly in the many canyons adjoining Firelane 10. The vegetative canopy produced by these large, old trees is highly beneficial for several reasons. The canopy of a thickly growing forest helps filter out pollutants created by automobile and industrial emissions. It moderates the effects of storms and wind and slows the runoff of precipitation, thus protecting downstream neighborhoods from flooding and landslides. The trees of Forest Park also act as a buffer against the noise produced by a rapidly growing urban area.

After approximately ¾ miles, Firelane 10 crosses over a sizeable creek, and proceeds uphill, at times at a steep angle. A half-mile further, Firelane 10 comes out at N.W. Germantown Road. At this juncture, turn right and walk a quarter mile uphill along Germantown Road, until its intersection with Wildwood Trail. Turn right again on Wildwood Trail and head north for .8 miles. Near Wildwood Milepost 25, the trail is intersected by Firelane 8, which comes in from above. Continue on Wildwood Trail and cross over a scenic creek, which cascades with runoff in winter and spring. This stream exemplifies the "intermittent creeks" that so frequently occur in Forest Park. Characteristically, these types of watersheds have well-defined, steeply-graded channels. In the wet seasons of the year, they can be charged with water. In summer they can be dry. Erosion and flood damage resulting from "flashy flows" occurring during the rainy months, are mitigated in Forest Park because of the luxuriant vegetative growth that borders these streams.

Just before Wildwood Milepost 25½, the trail crosses Firelane 10. Turn left on Firelane 10 and proceed .15 mile. Firelane 10 exits at the Newton Street parking area, completing the loop.

FIRELANE 7– HARDESTY TRAIL– RIDGE TRAIL LOOP

DISTANCE: 1.74 miles
HIKING TIME: 1 to 1½ hours
ELEVATION LOSS: 250 feet
ELEVATION GAIN: 275 feet
HIGH POINT: 1,025 feet
Firelane 7 open to foot traffic and horses only. Hardesty, Wildwood, and Ridge Trails allow foot traffic only.

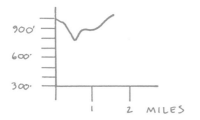

THIS MEDLEY OF INTERLINKING TRAILS, which in sections is steep and can be very slippery when wet, is still a very worthwhile hike. It winds through deep, quiet forests in the heart of Forest Park and always seems fragrant with the scent of spicy ferns and damp evergreen needles.

To reach the trailhead, drive west along N.W. Skyline Blvd. until its intersection with N.W. Springville Road. Drive past the west-leading portion of Springville Road (on your left) and drive a bit further to the east-leading portion. Turn right (east) on Springville Road, and follow it for about

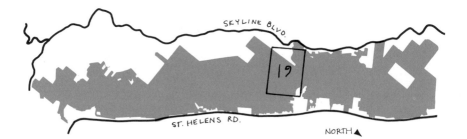

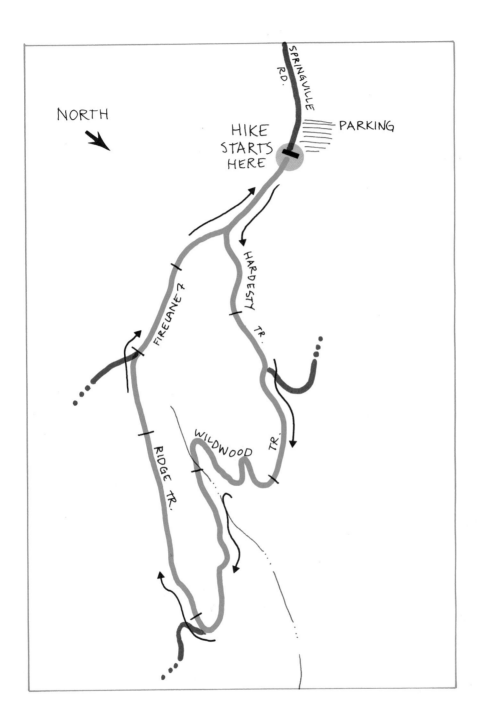

NORTH

SPRINGVILLE RD.

HIKE STARTS HERE

PARKING

HARDESTY TR.

FIRELANE 7

WILDWOOD TR.

RIDGE TR.

a half mile until it ends at a park gate. Here is a parking area, with room for cars as well as horse trailers.

Begin the hike by walking around the park gate and veering right at the intersection of Firelane 7 with Springville Road. Continue on Firelane 7 as it heads up then down a gentle slope. Firelane 7 is bordered by red alders and big leaf maples as well as a thriving understory of cedar and western hemlock trees. Along the trail, be sure to keep an eye open for deer tracks, which are especially noticeable in muddy spots in winter and spring. Black-tailed deer frequent Forest Park, but their tracks are often more visible than the animals themselves. These deer are not herd animals and seldom form large associations. Generally, they occur in small family groups or small groups of bucks. Their primary food, which occurs throughout Forest Park, is salal, red huckleberry, blackberry, and thimbleberry. Thimbleberry, a shrub three to eight feet tall, with soft maple-like leaves and red fruit similar to a raspberry, can be seen in spring, summer and fall growing in luxuriant patches along Firelane 7.

After .13 mile, Hardesty Trail joins Firelane 7 on the left. Turn left (north) on Hardesty Trail, and proceed carefully down the steep, narrow footpath. When this trail is wet in winter and spring, footing can be precarious. As a result of its very dampness, however, this trail abounds with mosses, lichens, and beautiful, native ferns. Several varieties of ferns can be observed along the trail, and are also common throughout the park. Forest Park's most abundant fern, sword fern, grows profusely under the big-leaf maples bordering the trail. Deer fern is found growing in locations where there is deep shade and the soil is wet. Licorice fern can be observed growing luxuriantly out of the thick moss on the trunks of large trees, primarily big leaf maples. Other beautiful, native ferns can also be observed in spots, and include lady ferns, spreading wood ferns, and, the most delicate of all, maidenhair ferns.

Wildwood Trail intersects Hardesty Trail after approximately a quarter mile. At this junction, turn right on Wildwood Trail and walk for a little over a half mile until reaching Wildwood Milepost 21. Here, Ridge Trail intersects Wildwood Trail. Turn right on Ridge Trail.

For most of Ridge Trail's .40 miles, the path is a gentle upgrade. Ridge Trail is aptly named; it follows along the top of a rise that drops off on either side into ravines dense with young deciduous and evergreen trees. The cheerful singing of winter wrens, song sparrows, kinglets, and chickadees often accompanies a hiker passing along this lovely little trail.

Ridge Trail ends at its junction with Firelane 7. Turn right on Firelane 7 and continue up the hill. At several spots along Firelane 7, snags – or standing dead trees – are visible. Some of these snags sport obvious signs of a pileated woodpecker's handiwork. Snags such as these are very important for cavity nesting birds who use these holes (excavated by woodpeckers) for their nesting sites. Throughout western coniferous forests, snags greater than 23 inches in diameter at breast height and over 65 feet tall are the most often used as nesting sites for cavity nesting, native birds.

Firelane 7 continues its upward climb for .37 miles. At this point, it joins Springville Road. The parking area is visible from here, and marks the end of the loop.

NEWTON STREET HIKE TWENTY

DISTANCE: 1.93 miles one way
HIKING TIME: Approximately 1 hour each way
ELEVATION LOSS: 800 feet
HIGH POINT: 900 feet
Foot, bicycle, and horse traffic are allowed.

THIS HIKE IS OFTEN DONE ROUND TRIP, as there is no safe parking available on Newton Street at its junction with busy U.S. 30 (St. Helen's Highway). To access the trailhead, drive northwest along N.W. Skyline Blvd. until its intersection with N.W. Newton Street, .5 mile north of Germantown Road. Turn right (east) onto Newton Street, and follow it .3 mile, until it dead ends at a well-defined parking area. The hike begins just to the north of the parking area and follows the continuation of Newton Street, which, from this point, is closed to all motorized traffic except official Park vehicles.

Newton Street is a vigorous hike, for the grass-covered pathway drops

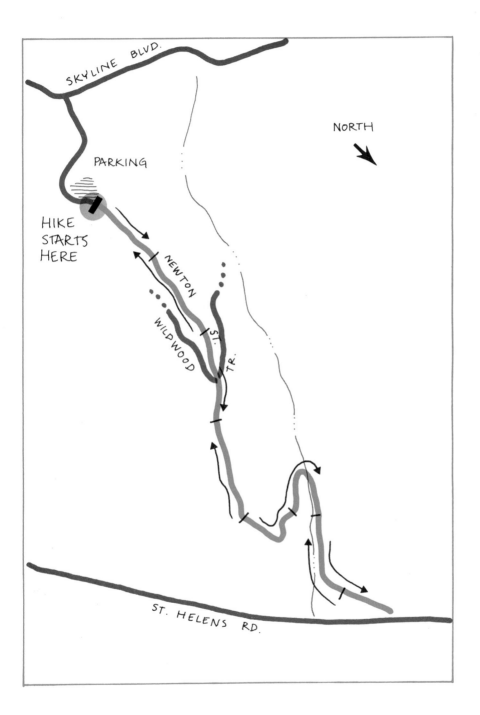

SKYLINE BLVD.

NORTH

PARKING

HIKE
STARTS
HERE

NEWTON ST.

WILDWOOD

TR.

ST. HELENS RD.

over 800 feet in elevation in just under two miles. Expending the effort to do the hike round trip, however, is well worth it. The trail winds through quiet, impressive groves of cedar and fern, as well as open, grassy areas frequented by black-tailed deer. Viewpoints through the trees along Newton Street provide panoramas of the Willamette River with its active shipping industry, and of Mt. Hood, Mt. St. Helens, Mt. Adams, and Mt. Rainier.

As the hike begins, the trail passes through a forest primarily made up of red alder, big leaf maple and Douglas fir trees. Newton Street is one of twelve firelanes that dissect Forest Park, generally in an east-west orientation, and running perpendicular to Skyline Blvd. Although these firelanes are closed to recreational vehicular traffic, they are continually maintained by the Portland Park Bureau and Fire Department to provide necessary access to remote sections of Forest Park in the case of wildfire.

After .6 mile, Newton Street crosses Wildwood Trail. Continue on Newton Street, and look north (left) of the trail for some fine examples of old growth Douglas fir trees. This area of Forest Park is one of only a few pockets where true old growth forest features can be observed. Under natural conditions, certain traits begin to be noticeable in forest stands that are over 175 years old. Huge trees that often have irregular crowns or broken tops and overtop the adjoining canopy are characteristic of old growth vegetation. In Forest Park, some Douglas fir giants reach up to 200 feet in height and range from 22 to 87 inches at diameter at breast height (dbh). Other structural attributes indicative of old growth habitat, and also observable in the ravines north of Newton Street, include the presence of large, standing dead trees (snags), and a prevalence of very large, dead and downed logs in various stages of decay.

As Newton Street continues winding downhill, it narrows in spots as it approaches closer to the Willamette River. Approximately a mile from the parking area where Newton Street crosses Wildwood Trail, notice to the south (right) a "Witness Post Survey Marker." These historic survey markers, eleven of which occur in Forest Park, refer to the original 1854 survey conducted by the U.S. Government for the region. Nineteenth-century surveyors recorded reference points to public land survey section-corners and described the natural vegetation of the area surrounding them. Today, the notes garnered by these earlier surveyors give important clues to the historic vegetation of an area. At this particular witness site off Newton Street, surveyors recorded that the vegetation was "burned, second rate timber," with fir trees measuring 18-36 inches dbh. Other witness posts in Forest Park, however, reveal a forest of large trees of Douglas fir and cedar with 40-60 inch dbh. An early Portland pioneer, Peter Burnett, also commented about the huge trees growing just southeast of Newton Street near the town of Linnton. In a letter he wrote to a friend in 1844, he stated "You can find them (fir trees) in the vicinity of Linnton from 8 feet in diameter to small saplings."

As Newton Street nears the Willamette, look through the trees for stunning views of majestic mountains. Along this grassy stretch, black-tailed deer tracks are often visible in the mud. This is a good spot to stop for a picnic lunch and to listen for resonant ship horns wafting up from the river.

Beyond this stretch, two locked, park gates mark the eastern boundary of Newton Street at its intersection with St. Helen's Highway (Highway 30). Off-road parking is not safe here because of the high traffic volume on the highway. Conclude the hike by retracing steps up Newton Street and return to the parking area.

FOREST PARK TOMORROW

A S THE PORTLAND METROPOLITAN AREA continues to grow, Forest Park becomes increasingly
important for its recreational, educational, and aesthetic
values.

The richness of the park, with its array of native wildlife and plants, brings the western coniferous ecosystem
right into the heart of the city of Portland. Today, a person learning about the vegetation, birds, and mammals of
Forest Park can travel to other low elevation Douglas fir
forests in western Oregon and Washington and be familiar with the naturally occurring flora and fauna.

For this privilege to continue to exist – and indeed it is
a privilege – it will be necessary to retain suitable habitat
conditions for Forest Park's wildlife. Large blocks of unbroken forest habitat, snags, downed logs, and old growth
areas must be maintained for those species requiring such
features. Additionally and perhaps most importantly, it
will be necessary to insure that the park is not one day
surrounded on all sides by encroaching urban sprawl.

If the corridor of natural habitat that presently connects the park to more rural areas of the Coast Range is
eliminated, the wildlife diversity that we know today in
Forest Park will dramatically decline. Private holdings
within the park also threaten the future of Forest Park.
These areas need to become a part of the park, as was
originally intended from the master plans drawn up by
the Olmstead Brothers, Robert Moses, the City Club,
the Forest Park Committee of Fifty (today known as
"Friends of Forest Park"), the City Council, and, most
recently, by Portland Parks and Recreation and the Bureau of Planning.

Forest Park has been blessed by the tireless advocacy of many individuals who have worked for nearly one hundred years to protect its extraordinary natural qualities. Today, this vigilance and concern still continues. Since 1990, the Friends of Forest Park has worked with numerous private land owners to negotiate conservation easements on properties surrounding the park to buffer the park from intensive, surrounding development. The Friends of Forest Park also spearheaded a remarkable grassroots campaign to raise $700,000 to save Portland's last stand of old growth forest, a thirty-eight acre parcel near Forest Park's northern boundary, and to purchase conservation easements on several hundred additional acres within the wildlife corridor. Other plans are currently being developed to link Portland with the Pacific Coast, via "The Pacific Greenway." An extension of Forest Park's Wildwood Trail may one day form an integral piece of this greenway network.

For its naturalness, beauty, and remarkable history, Forest Park is unquestionably Portland's quiet treasure. Those who love it hope that it will continue to stand with dignity and grace, a living testimony to one city's wise and visionary planning, for countless future generations.

FRIENDS OF FOREST PARK

FRIENDS OF FOREST PARK is a nonprofit citizens' organization dedicated to enhancing and preserving Forest Park in the heart of our city. The Friends are stewards of the Park and advocates for its sustained presence as a source of enrichment in the greater Portland metropolitan community. Through its citizen members, the Friends inform the public about Forest Park, aid in its management, and sponsor educational and recreational activities.

The Friends Board of Directors, and interested members, meet monthly with the Portland Bureau of Parks and Recreation—working together to assure effective implementation of the Forest Park Management Plan. If you appreciate Forest Park, and enjoy its presence, you can help sustain it for today and for future generations. Become a member of Friends of Forest Park.

Friends of Forest Park
P.O. Box 2413
Portland, OR 97208
223-5449

BIBLIOGRAPHY

Adams, L.W. and L.E. Dove. 1989. *Wildlife Reserves and Corridors in the Urban Environment: a Guide to Ecological Landscape Planning and Resource Conservation*. National Institute for Urban Wildlife, Columbia, MD.

Adams, L.W. and D.L. Leedy, eds. 1987. *Integrating Man and Nature in the Metropolitan Environment*. National Institute for Urban Wildlife, Columbia, MD.

Bennett, E. H. *The Greater Portland Plan*. Portland, 1912.

Burgess, R.C. and D.M. Sharp, eds. 1891. *Forest Island Dynamics in Man-dominated Landscapes*. Springer-Verlag, New York.

Cline, S. P., et al. "Snag Characteristics in Douglas Fir Forests, Western Oregon." *Journal of Wildlife Management*, 44. 1980: 773-86.

Davis, A. M., and T. F. Glick. "Urban Ecosystems and Island Biogeography." *Environmental Conservation*, 5. 1978: 299-304.

Diamond, J.M. 1975. "The Island Dilemma: Lessons of Modern Biogeographic Studies for the Design of Natural Preserves." *Biological Conservation*. 7:129-146.

Forest Park Committee. 1976. "A Management Plan for Forest Park." (As further revised by Council action Nov. 10, 1976, and amended by Friends of Forest Park, Dec. 21, 1989.) Portland, OR.

Franklin, J. F., et al. *Ecological Characteristics of Old-growth Douglas Fir Forests*. USDA Forest Service General Technical Report. PNW-118. 1981.

———, et al. *Natural Vegetation of Oregon and Washington*. USDA Forest Service General Technical Report. PNW-8. 1980.

Harris, L.D. 1984. *The Fragmented Forest–Island Biogeography Theory and the Preservation of Biotic Diversity*. University of Chicago Press.

——— 1988. "Landscape Linkages: the Dispersal Corridor Approach to Wildlife Conservation." *Transactions of the North American Wildlife Natural Resource Conference*. 53:595-607.

Hitchcock, C. L., and A. Cronquist. *Flora of the Pacific Northwest*. Seattle, 1978.

Houle, M.C. 1990. "Wild About The City: Phase One of the West Hills Wildlife Corridor Study." Prepared for the Multnomah County Division of Planning and Development.

Keil, B. *Guide to the Roads and Trails of Forest Park*. Portland, 1973.

Lewis, M., and W. Clark. *The Lewis and Clark Expedition*. Vol. 3, Edited by Nicholas Biddle. New York, 1961.

MacClintock, L., R. F. Whitcomb, and B.L. Whitcomb. 1977. "Island Biogeography and 'Habitat Islands' of Eastern Forests. Evidence For the Value of Corridors and Minimization of Isolation in Preservation of Biotic Diversity." *American Birds*. 31:6-12.

Mackintosh, G. ed. 1989. *Preserving Communities and Corridors*. Washington, D.C.

Mannan. R. W., et al. "Use of Snags by Birds in Douglas Fir Forests, Western Oregon." *Journal of Wildlife Management*, 44. 1980: 787-97.

Maser, C., et al. *Natural History of Oregon Coast Mammals*. USDA Forest Service General Technical Report. PNW-133. 1981.

Meslow. E. C. "The Relationship of Birds of Habitat Structure–Plant Communities and Successional Stages." *Proceedings of the Workshop on Nongame Bird Habitat Management in the Coniferous Forests of the Western United States*. Edited by R. DeGraff. USDA Forest Service General Technical Report. PNW-64. 1978: 12-18.

Moses, Robert. *Portland Improvement*. Report to the Portland City Council. Portland, 1943.

Munger, T. T. *History of Portland's Forest Park*. Portland, 1960.

Newton, M., et al. "Role of Alder in Western Oregon Forest Succession." *Biology of Alder*. Edited by J. M. Trappe, et al. Pacific Northwest Forest and Range Experiment Station. 1967: 73-84.

Noss, R.F. 1987. "Protection Natural Areas in Fragmented Landscapes." *Natural Areas Journal*. 7:2-13.

Olmstead, J. C., and F. L. Olmstead, Jr. *Report of the Park Board*. Portland, 1903.

Pintarich, Dick. "The Portland That Might Have Been." *Oregon Magazine*. Aug. 1979: 53-60.

Portland Parks and Recreation; Bureau of Planning. 1995. "Forest Park: Natural Resources Management Plan." Adopted by City Council February 8, 1995.

Robbins, C. S., et al. *Birds of North America*. New York, 1983.

Soule, M. 1986. "Conservation Biology–the Science of Scarcity and Diversity." Sinauer Assoc. Sunderland, Mass.

Sullivan, R. 1989. "Tying the Landscape Together: the Need for Wildlife Movement Corridors." Cooperative Extension Service, University of Florida.

Trimble, D. E., "Geology of Portland, Oregon and Adjacent Areas." *Geological Survey Bulletin.* 1119. 1963.

Warren, C. E., et al. "Conceptual Frameworks and Philosophical Foundations of General Living Systems Theory." *Behavioral Science,* 24. 1979: 296-310.

Wilcove, D.S. 1987. "From Fragmentation to Extinction." *Natural Areas Journal.* 7: 23-29.

Wilcox, B.A. and D.D. Murphy. 1985. "Conservation Strategy: the Effects of Fragmentation on Extinction." *American Naturalist.* 125: 879-887.

Wilson, E.O. 1988. *Biodiversity.* National Academy Press. Washington, D.C.

ILLUSTRATION LIST

Photographs

INDEX

COLOPHON

THE TYPEFACE used for both text and display in *One City's Wilderness: Portland's Forest Park* is Sabon. The last typeface designed by one of the twentieth century's foremost designers, Jan Tschichold, Sabon was commissioned by German master printers to meet specific pre-photocomposition-era technical requirements. The goal was to create a "harmonized" typeface with identical forms for mechanical (Monotype and Linotype) and foundry composition. It was later successfully adapted for digital composition. The successful resultant face, Sabon, is highly readable and pleasing to the eye.

Production of this volume was accomplished through the skill and cooperation of the following:

Typesetting: Irish Setter, Portland
Printing–map: Irwin-Hodson, Portland
Printing–book: Paramount Graphics, Portland
Interior book design: George Resch
Cover design: Martha Gannett
Hike maps, pen and ink illustrations: Christine Rains
Forest Park map, locator maps: Martha Gannett
Trillium illustrations: Connie Barnes
Cover photo: Ron Cronin

ABOUT THE AUTHOR

MARCY HOULE, an award winning author and wildlife biologist, was hired as an ecological consultant to study Forest Park intensively for several years. She is the author of *Wings For My Flight*, and *The Prairie Keepers*. Mrs. Houle lives in Portland, Oregon, with her husband and two young daughters–avid hikers who assisted her in her explorations of all the trails described in this book.